THE MIRACLE
OF THE JEWS

THE MIRACLE OF THE JEWS

ROBERT H. SCHRAM

To order additional copies of this book, contact:
Xlibris
844-714-8691
www.Xlibris.com
Orders@Xlibris.com
842706

Contents

Introduction

As a Jew whose DNA is 97% Ashkenazi Jewish and 3% Middle Eastern my blood line must have originated from Patriarch Abraham and Matriarch Sarah! I was touched deeply to learn more about my people since although I believe in our Blessed Creator I found it exceedingly difficult to believe that the Creator of an incomprehensible infinite universe would have any particular concern with one small star in a universe with multibillions of stars, let alone even more billions of planets that orbit these stars, let alone of all the millions of species of life on one tiny orb (earth), the Creator would have any particular concern with the highest sentient species (humans), let alone a tiny tribe of his believers from the lineage of a man named Abraham. After many years of study and research I was moved to write this book since the only logical conclusion I have come to is:

Our Blessed Creator of our incomprehensible infinite universe does acknowledge one of multibillions of stars (our sun), and one of the smallest planets in orbit around this sun (earth), and the highest sentient species (humans) on this planet, and those in the lineage of Abraham and Sarah.

I believed that the miracles in the Jewish Tenach (an acronym for *Torah*, *Nevi'im* -'Prophets', and *Ketuvim* – 'Writings' ergo TaNaKh) were stories that teach rather than actual happenings: staffs turning into snakes and consuming other snakes, looking at a snake to be cured, plagues devastating only Egyptians, the splitting of seas, talking asses, and stopping time among many others. However, I cannot, nor can anyone else deny the miracles we have witnessed since the end of World War II. The rebirth of the state of Israel in 1948 was a miracle of history (Ezek.37:1-11; Luke 21:29,30). Never in human history has a nation been destroyed, its people dispersed to the ends of the earth, and then, nearly two thousand years later, re-gather to their homeland, build a nation with a conversational language (Hebrew) re-born as the national language.

On January 16, 1996, then President of Israel, Ezer Weizmann, gave a speech to both Houses of Parliament of Germany. He gave this speech in Hebrew to the Germans, fifty years after the Holocaust. It sums up what Jewish history is:

> *It was fate that delivered me and my contemporaries into this great era when the Jews returned to re-establish their homeland ...*
>
> *I am no longer a wandering Jew who migrates from country to country, from exile to exile. But all Jews in every generation must regard themselves as if they had been there in previous generations, places, and events. Therefore, I am still a wandering Jew but not along the far-flung paths of the world. Now I migrate through the expanses of time from generation to generation down the paths of memory ...*
>
> *I was a slave in Egypt. I received the Torah on Mount Sinai. Together with Joshua and Elijah I crossed the Jordan River. I entered Jerusalem with David and was exiled with Zedekiah. And I did not forget it by the rivers of*

Babylon. When the Lord returned the captives of Zion I dreamed among the builders of its ramparts. I fought the Romans and was banished from Spain. I was bound to the stake in Mainz. I studied Torah in Yemen and lost my family in Kishinev. I was incinerated in Treblinka, rebelled in Warsaw, and emigrated to the Land of Israel, the country from where I have been exiled and where I have been born and from which I come and to which I return.

I am a wandering Jew who follows in the footsteps of my forebearers. And just as I escort them there and now and then, so do my forebearers accompany me and stand with me here today.

I am a wandering Jew with the cloak of memory around my shoulders and the staff of hope in my hand. I stand at the great crossroads in time, at the end of the twentieth century. I know whence I come and with hope and apprehension I attempt to find out where I am heading.

<blockquote>

We are all people of memory and prayer. We are people of words and hope. We have neither established empires nor built castles and palaces. We have only placed words on top of each other. We have fashioned ideas. We have built memorials. We have dreamed towers of yearning, of Jerusalem rebuilt, of Jerusalem united, of a peace that will swiftly and speedily establish us in our days. Amen.[1]

</blockquote>

The very survival of the Jewish people through recorded time is miraculous and to some, supernatural. The only explanation that Jews exist as a nation today is a Creator who is active in earth's history. By any historical measure, the Jewish people should have disappeared long ago.

Israel's first Prime Minister David Ben Gurion said:

<blockquote>

A Jew who does not believe in miracles is not a realist.

</blockquote>

Miracles and/or supernatural acts are the only possible explanation for the existence of the Jewish people. Over 300 years ago King Louis XIV of France asked Blaise Pascal, the great French philosopher, to give him proof of the supernatural. Pascal answered in the 17th century CE:

> *Why, the Jews, your Majesty -- the Jews.*

Mark Twain (aka Samuel Clemens), the great American writer, who was an agnostic and a self-acknowledged skeptic, penned this in 1899 in *Harper's Magazine*:

> *If the statistics are right, the Jews constitute but one percent of the human race. It suggests a nebulous dim puff of star dust lost in the blaze of the Milky Way. Properly the Jew ought hardly be heard of; but he is heard of, has always been heard of.*
>
> *He is as prominent on the planet as any other people, and his commercial importance is extravagantly out of proportion to the smallness of his bulk. His contributions to the world's list of great names in literature, science, art, music, finance, medicine, and abstruse learning are also way out of proportion to the weakness of his numbers. He has made a marvelous fight in this world, in all ages; and has done it with his hands tied behind*

him. He could be vain of himself and be excused for it.

The Egyptian, the Babylonian, and the Persian rose, filled the planet with sound and splendor, then faded to dream-stuff and passed away. The Greek and Roman followed, made a vast noise and they are gone. Other peoples have sprung up, and held their torch high for a time, but it burned out and they sit in twilight now or have vanished. The Jew saw them all, beat them all, and is now what he always was, exhibiting no decadence, no infirmities of age, no weakening of his parts, no slowing of his energies, no dulling of his alert and aggressive mind. All things are mortal, but the Jew. All other forces pass, but he remains. What is the secret of his immortality?

Leo Nikolaivitch Tolstoy, unlike Twain, was a deeply religious Russian Orthodox Christian. He is also a famous Russian author from the last century, perhaps best known for *War and Peace* written in 1908:

What is a Jew? This question is not at all odd as it seems. Let us see what kind of peculiar creature the Jew is, which all the rulers and all nations have together and separately abused and molested, oppressed and persecuted, trampled and butchered, burned and hanged and in spite of all this is yet alive!

What is a Jew, who has never allowed himself to be led astray by all the earthly possessions which his oppressors and persecutors constantly offered him in order that he should change his faith and forsake his own Jewish religion?

The Jew is that sacred being who has brought down from heaven the everlasting fire and has illumined with it the entire world. He is the religious source, spring, and fountain out of which all the rest of the peoples have drawn their beliefs and their religions.

The Jew is the pioneer of liberty. Even in those olden days, when the people were divided into but two distinct classes, slaves and masters even so long ago had the law of Moses prohibited the practice of keeping a person in bondage for more than six years.

The Jew is the pioneer of civilization. Ignorance was condemned in olden Palestine more even than it is today in civilized Europe. Moreover, in those wild and barbarous days, when neither life nor the death of anyone counted for anything at all, Rabbi Akiba did not refrain from expressing himself openly against capital punishment, a practice which is recognized today as a highly civilized way of punishment.

The Jew is the emblem of civil and religious toleration. "Love the stranger and the sojourner", Moses commands, because you have been strangers in the land of Egypt.

And this was said in those remote and savage times when the principal ambition of the races and nations consisted in crushing and enslaving one another. As concerns religious toleration, the Jew is not only far from the missionary spirit of converting people of other denominations, but on the contrary, the Talmud commands the Rabbis to inform and explain to everyone who willingly comes to accept the Jewish religion, all the difficulties involved in its acceptance, and to point out to the would-be proselyte that the righteous of all nations have a share in immortality (heaven). Of such a lofty and ideal religious toleration not even the moralists of our present day can boast.

The Jew is the emblem of eternity. He who neither slaughter nor torture of thousands of years could destroy, he who neither fire, nor sword, nor Inquisition was able to wipe off the face of the earth. He who was the first to produce the Oracles of God. He who has been for so long the Guardian of Prophecy and has transmitted it to the rest of the world. Such a nation cannot be destroyed. The Jew is as everlasting as Eternity itself.[2]

Phyllis Bottome English novelist, 1938 said:

To be a Jew is to be strong with a strength that has outlived persecutions. It is to be wise against ignorance, honest against piracy, harmless against evil, kind against cruelty.

Joseph Priestly English scientist/founder of Unitarianism, 1794 said:

It pleased God to make one nation the medium of all His communications with mankind: This the nation of the Jews has done to a considerable degree in all ages as civilization extended, they by one means or another became most wonderfully dispersed through all countries; and at this day they are almost literally everywhere, the most conspicuous, and in the eye of reason and religion, the most respectable nation on the face of the earth.

John Adams *American* President, 1809 said:

The Hebrews have done more to civilize men than any other nation: The doctrine of a supreme, intelligent sovereign of the universe, I believe to be the great essential principle of all morality, and consequently of all civilization.

Antonio Rubiero Santos, *early* nineteenth century Portuguese jurist said:

> *We are largely indebted to the Jews for our first knowledge of philosophy, botany, medicine, astronomy, cosmography, (the nature of the universe), the sacred languages, and almost all branches of biblical study.*

Thomas B. MacCaulay English statesman, 1833 said:

> *In the infancy of civilization, when our island was as savage as New Guinea, when letters and arts were still unknown to Athens, when scarcely a thatched roofed hut stood on what was later the site of Rome, this contemned people had their fenced cities and cedar palaces, their splendid Temple, their fleets of merchant ships, their schools of sacred learning, their great statesmen and soldiers, their natural philosophers, their historians and their poets.*

Lyman Abbott early 19th century American preacher and journalist said:

> *We Gentiles owe our life to Israel. It is Israel who has brought us the message that God is one, and that God is a just and righteous God, and demands righteousness of his children It is Israel that has brought us the message that God is our Father. It is Israel who, in bringing us the divine law, has laid the foundation of liberty. It is Israel who had the first free institutions the world ever saw. When our own unchristian prejudices flame out against the Jewish people, let us remember that all that we have and all that we are we owe, under God, to what Judaism has given us.[2]*

T. H. Huxley biologist and religious controversialist, 1892 said:

> *Throughout the history of the Western world, the Scriptures have been the great instigators of revolt against the worst forms of religious and political despotism.*

> *The Bible has been the Magna Charta of the poor and of the oppressed;*

down to modern times, no State has had a constitution in which the interest of the people are so largely taken into account, in which the duties so much more than the privileges of rulers are insisted upon, as that drawn up for Israel in Deuteronomy and in Leviticus; nowhere is the fundamental truth that the welfare of the State, in the long run, depends on the uprightness of the citizen strongly laid down. The Bible is the most democratic book in the world.[3]

Poet Eva wrote *Israel a Miracle* Jerusalem Post 8-23-1998:

> *...They gave up their old lives in*
> *Exchange for the new, and*
> *Israel prospered and Israel grew,*
> *Where she stands a reminder to both*
> *Gentile and Jew: A miracle.*

The Eternal Riddle by Philip M. Raskin

> *...Pray, has thy saga*
> *Likewise an ending,*
> *As its beginning*
> *Glorious of old*

Less miraculous reasons for Jewish survival has to do with religion. The Sabbath especially in the diasporas throughout history has helped Jewish survival. Regardless of the levels of persecution, pogroms, exiles, conversions, and mass murders once every week Jewish families were able to celebrate and bless God together. The annual Passover celebration which is also celebrated in each families' home reminds Jews of their incredible survival history. The more families have connected to Judaism, the more likely that their children and grandchildren would remain Jewish and not assimilate into the gentile mainstream of humanity.

Due to persecution and assimilation, there are only about 14 million Jews in the world instead of about 500 million. The greatest strength of the Jewish people is also their greatest weakness. God has called Jews a *stiff-necked* people. They have stubbornly held onto their beliefs and as a result outlasted all the ancient empires of history while changing the way the entire world looks at morality and the concept of God. Jewish strength of character can also be Jews' greatest weakness. Their stubborn individuality makes them unbendable.

Abraham, Isaac, and Jacob

Observant Jewish belief is that the Hebrew year from Creation is 5782 (2022 on the Gregorian Calendar) which means we have 218 more years to arrive at our final destination...the Messianic Age. The rationale for this belief is that the first 6,000 years of Creation is like the work week before the Sabbath; six days of work and a day of rest symbolic of the Messianic Age. That Age was described by Prophet Isaiah (2:4) in these words:

> In the days to come, The Mount of the Lord's House shall stand Firm above the mountains; And it shall tower above the hills. And all the nations shall gaze on it with joy, And the many peoples shall go and shall say:
>
> 'Come, let us go up to the Mount of the Lord, To the House of the God

of Jacob; That He may instruct us in His ways, And that we may walk in His paths.' For instruction shall come forth from Zion, The word of the Lord from Jerusalem. Thus, He will judge among the many people. And arbitrate for the multitude of nations. And they shall beat their swords into plowshares and their spears into pruning hooks. Nations shall not take up Sword against nation; They shall never again know war.

Abraham, the Patriarch of Judaism, Christianity, and Islam was believed to have been born in Ur, Chaldea c 1819 BCE and believed to have died at age 175 in Hebron, Shaam c 1644 BCE. God calls on Abraham to leave the idolatrous house of his father Terah (the ninth in descent from Noah) and settle in Canaan, a land He promises for Abraham's progeny. Abraham's second son Isaac by 90-year-old wife Sarah inherits God's promised land, not first son Ishmael by handmaiden Hagar...whose future progeny contains many Middle Eastern Arabs. The Cave of the Patriarchs at Hebron was purchased by Abraham thus establishing his right to the land. Abraham marries Keturah and had six more sons; but, on his death, after being buried beside Sarah at The Cave of the Patriarchs, it is Isaac who receives "all Abraham's goods", while the other sons receive only "gifts". (Genesis 25:5–8) Abram, nephew Lot, and their households went to Egypt when famine struck in Canaan. Fearing for his life Abram told the Egyptians Sarah was his sister and the Pharaoh gave Abram goods in exchange for her. When finding out the truth both Abram and Sarah were expelled from Egypt. (Gen 12:10-20)

Abram and Lot's sizable herds occupied the same pastures causing conflicts, so each herd was taken to separate pastures. Lot's herd dwelled in cities of the plain toward Sodom while Abram's herd went south to Hebron and settled in the plain of Mamre. Abram was told nephew Lot and his family were prisoners of the Elamite forces. He assembled 318 trained servants and attacked at night in the Battle of Siddim defeating the Elamites and slaughtering their King Chedorlaomer while freeing all the captives and their possessions. (Gen 14: 1-16)

In a vision God spoke to Abram promising descendants as numerous as the stars owning the land of the Kenites, Kenizzites, Kadmonites, Hittites, Perizzites, Rephaims, Amorites, Canaanites, Girgashites, and Jebusites. (Gen 15:1-21) When Abram was 99 years of age, God declared Abram's new name: "Abraham – a father of many nations" and he received instructions for the covenant with circumcision as the sign. (Gen 17:5-14)

Abraham, the gracious host washed the feet and fed three men by the terebinths of Mamre. One of the visitors told Abraham that Sarah would have a son the next year. (Gen 18:1-8) They discussed the fate of Sodom and Gomorrah for their detestable sins. God told Abraham that He would spare the city if at least ten righteous people were found which did not happen and the city was destroyed. (Gen 18: 17-33)

Abraham settled between Kadesh and Shur in the land of the Philistines. While living in Gerar, Abraham again claimed that Sarah was his sister and like the Pharaoh in Egypt, King Abimelech had Sarah brought to him. God then came to Abimelech in a dream and declared that taking her would result in death because she was a man's wife. Abimelech had not laid hands on her, and Abraham defended what he had said as not being a lie at all: *And yet indeed she is my sister; she is the daughter of my father, but not the daughter of my mother; and she became my wife.* (Gen 20:12) Abimelech returned Sarah to Abraham, and gave him gifts of sheep, oxen, and servants and invited him to settle wherever he pleased in Abimelech's lands. Further, Abimelech gave Abraham a thousand pieces of silver to serve as Sarah's vindication before all.

After Sarah told Abraham to send Hagar and Ishmael away so Isaac would inherit his father's property, God reassured Abraham that *in Isaac shall seed be called to thee*. He also said that Ishmael would make a nation *because he is thy seed*. (Gen 21:9-13) The two wandered in the wilderness of Beersheba until they were without water and an angel of the Lord confirmed to Hagar that from Ishmael would come a great nation, and will be *living on his sword*. Miraculously a well of water appeared saving their lives. Ishmael became a skilled archer living in the wilderness of Paran. Eventually his mother found a wife for Ishmael from her home country, the land of Egypt. (Gen 21: 14-21)

At some point in Isaac's life (rabbinic tradition puts his age at 37), God commanded Abraham to sacrifice his son in the land of Moriah. As they approached Mt. Moriah after traveling three days Isaac asked where the sacrificial animal was? Abraham replied that *God will provide a lamb for a burnt offering*. One of God's angels interrupted as Isaac was about to be sacrificed and Abraham saw behind him a *ram caught in a thicket by his horns*, which he sacrificed instead of his son. (Gen 22:1-19)

Isaac's name means *he will laugh* reflecting his laughter in disbelief, when God told his parents that they would birth a child in their old age. He was the father of Jacob, and the grandfather of the twelve tribes of Israel. He never moved out of Canaan and was the longest-lived patriarch dying at 180 years of life. Abraham sent his steward Eliezer to Mesopotamia before Isaac was 40 to find his wife to be, Rebekah who for many years was barren until birthing the twins Esau (favored by Isaac) and Jacob (favored by Rebekah) when Isaac was 60. (Gen 17: 15-19)

When the land at *Beer-lahai-roi* experienced famine, Isaac and family moved to the Philistine land of Gerar where his father once lived, still under the control of King Abimelech. Isaac, like his father deceived Abimelech about his wife and also got into the well business unearthing Abraham's wells covered with soil by the Philistines. He also dug more wells all the way to Beersheba and made a pact with the King as did his father. (Gen 26)

When Isaac was old and blind, his son went hunting for venison as directed by his father. Rebekah told Jacob to pretend to be Esau to obtain Isaac's blessing while Esau was out hunting. According to Genesis 25:29–34, Esau had previously sold his birthright to Jacob for *bread and stew of lentils*. Isaac sent Jacob into Mesopotamia to take a wife of his mother's brother's house. After 20 years working for his uncle Laban, Jacob returned home. He reconciled with his twin brother Esau, then he and Esau buried their father, Isaac in Hebron at age 180. (Gen 35: 28-29) According to local tradition, the graves of Isaac and Rebekah, along with the graves of Abraham and Sarah and Jacob and Leah, are in the Cave of the Patriarchs.

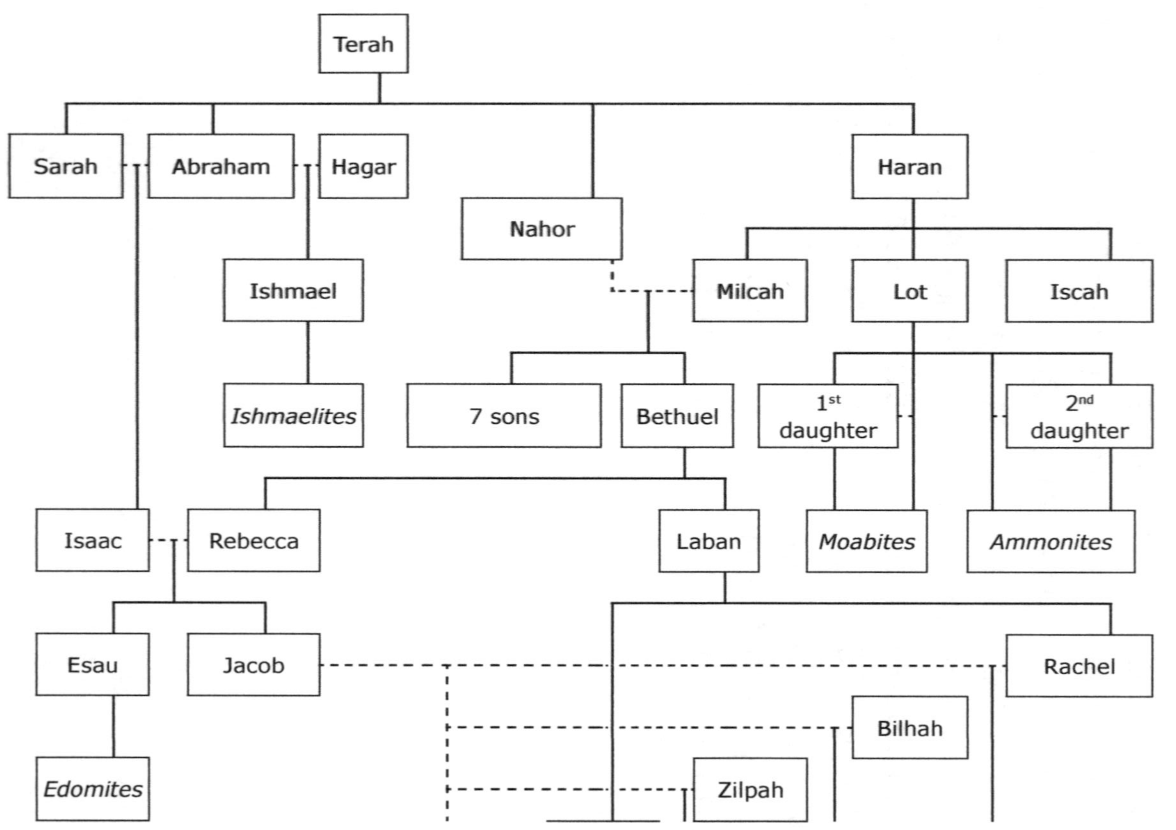

Terah
Sarah
Abraham
Hagar
Haran
Nahor
Ishmael
Milcah
Lot
Iscah
Ishmaelites
7 sons
Bethuel
1st daughter
2nd daughter
Isaac
Rebecca
Laban
Moabites
Ammonites
Esau
Jacob
Rachel
Bilhah
Zilpah
Edomites

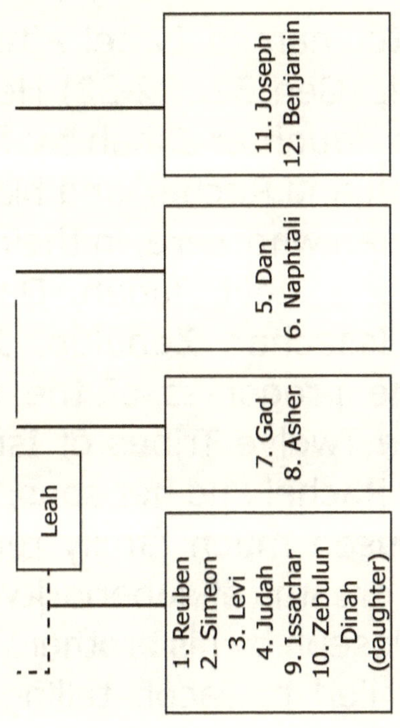

Leah
11. Joseph
12. Benjamin
5. Dan
6. Naphtali
7. Gad
8. Asher
1. Reuben
2. Simeon
3. Levi
4. Judah
9. Issachar
10. Zebulun
Dinah
(daughter)

According to the Jewish tradition, Isaac instituted the afternoon prayer based on Genesis 24:63: *Isaac went out to meditate in the field at the eventide.*

Jacob was later named Israel after struggling with an angel. (Gen 32: 22-32) He had twelve sons and one daughter Dinah by four women, his wives, Leah and Rachel, and his concubines Bilhah and Zilpah who were, in their birth order: Reuben, Simeon, Levi, Judah, Dan, Naphtali, Gad, Asher, Issachar, Zebulun, Joseph, and Benjamin. The progenies of the twelve sons comprised the Twelve Tribes of Israel. Jacob's favoritism for Rachel and her sons, Joseph, and Benjamin, caused much family tension, along with Joseph's dreams of superiority culminating in the sale of Joseph by his brothers into slavery. The brothers lied to Jacob telling him a wild animal killed Joseph when in fact they gave him to a caravan as a slave headed for Egypt. (Genesis 37:36)

Jacob had a vision of a ladder, or staircase, reaching into heaven with angels going up and down ("Jacob's ladder") and the voice of God heard from the top of the ladder. According to Midrash Genesis Rabbah, the ladder signified the exiles that the Jewish people would suffer before the coming of the Jewish Messiah: the angels represented the exiles of Babylonia, Persia, and Greece and each climbed up a certain number of steps, paralleling the years of the exile, before they "fell down"; but the angel representing the last exile, that of Edom kept climbing higher and higher into the clouds. The progenitor of the Edomites was Esau. Jacob feared that his descendants would never be free of Esau's domination, but God assured him that at the End of Days, Edom too would come falling down.[4]

Jacob arrived in Haran and saw the Amamean Laban and his daughter and first cousin, Rachel. Laban said he must work seven years for him before marrying Rachel. Seven years past and Laban deceived him by switching Rachel for her older veiled sister Leah. To marry Rachel Jacob agreed to work another seven years. He loved Rachel more than Leah, and Leah felt it. Leah rapidly gave birth to four sons: Reuben, Simeon, Levi, and Judah. Following Sarah's example barren Rachel gave her handmaid Bilah to Jacob who birthed Dan and Naphtali. Leah then gave her handmaid Zilpah to Jacob who birthed Gad and Asher. Leah became fertile again and gave birth to Issachar, Zebulun, and Dinah. God remembered Rachel, who gave birth to Joseph and Benjamin.

After Joseph was born, Jacob decided to return home to his parents. After more Laban treachery Jacob and his clan left and Rachel stole Laban's *teraphim* (household idols) from his house.

Laban pursued and caught up with Jacob confronting him and asking him to return the stolen *teraphim*. The theft unknown to Jacob was hidden by Rachel and Laban returned home and Jacob's clan continued their journey back to Canaan.

As Jacob neared the land of Canaan, brother Esau was coming to meet him with an army of 400 men. Jacob sent a tribute of flocks and herds to Esau. When Jacob was alone, a mysterious being appeared (man in Genesis 32:24, 28; or God in Genesis 32:28, 30, Hosea 12:3, 5; or angel in Hosea 12:4), and the two wrestled until daybreak. The being when not overpowering Jacob, touched him on the sinew of his thigh (the *gid hanasheh*), resulting in the development of a limp. (Genesis 32:31) The people of Israel do not eat the sinew of the thigh that is on the hip socket. (Genesis 32:32) After struggling with the mysterious being Jacob became known as Israel meaning he struggled with the divine angel.

Esau's spirit of revenge was apparently appeased by Jacob's bounteous gifts of camels, goats, and flocks. Their reunion was an emotional one.

Jacob then arrived in Shechem and bought a parcel of land, now identified as Joseph's Tomb. In Shechem, Jacob's daughter Dinah was kidnapped and raped by the ruler's son, who desired to marry the girl. Dinah's brothers, Simeon, and Levi, agreed in Jacob's name to permit the marriage if all the men of Shechem first circumcised themselves. On the third day after the circumcisions, when all the men of Shechem were still in pain, Simeon and Levi put them all to death by the sword and rescued their sister Dinah, and their brothers plundered the property, women, and children. Jacob condemned this act and later rebuked his two sons for their anger in his deathbed blessing. (Genesis 49:5–7)

A severe Middle East famine twenty years later, lasted seven years. Only Egypt was prospering, and Jacob sent the ten sons of Leah, Bilhah, and Zilpah to buy Egyptian grain. Israel's youngest son Benjamin stayed behind by his father's order to keep him safe. (Genesis 42:1–5)

Nine sons returned stockpiled with grain on their donkeys with brother Simeon held prisoner until brother Benjamin was brought back to Egypt. Israel was angry with the loss of Joseph, Simeon, and now possibly Benjamin. (Genesis 42:26–38) Joseph, identified his brothers in Egypt and secretly returned the grain money to them on their donkeys. After consuming all the grain, they were sent back to Egypt to buy more accompanied by brother Benjamin, gifts, and double the money from the first purchase. (Genesis 43:1–14) When they returned from the second trip with 20 additional donkeys and transport wagons they told Israel that Joseph was alive and governor of Egypt. (Genesis 45:16–28) Israel and his entire house of 70, took their livestock and journeyed to Egypt. They were directed to disembark at Goshen and Jacob saw his son Joseph again after 22 years. Israel then said, *Now let me die, since I have seen your face, because you are still alive.* (Genesis 46:1–30) They met the Pharaoh and were welcomed to live in Goshen. (Genesis 46:31–47:28)

Israel (Jacob) was 147 years old when he called to his favorite son Joseph and pleaded that he not be buried in Egypt. Joseph's two sons, Ephraim and Manasseh became heirs to the inheritance of the house of Israel with their uncles (the other sons of Jacob). Israel called all his sons in and prophesied their blessings or curses to all twelve of them in order of their ages. (Genesis 47:29–49:32) Israel was buried with the other patriarchs in the Cave of Machpelah.

Egyptian Bondage and Exodus

Approximately 300 years passed from the birth of Abram to the death of Jacob in Egypt. The families grew in number and a different Egyptian pharaoh who had no memory of how Joseph had saved Egypt from famine and was fearful that the Israelites could become a threat to Egypt. He enslaved them and ordered the killing of all newborn Hebrew males. One baby is saved by being put into an ark of bulrushes on the Nile River. Pharaoh's daughter finds the child, and names him Moses raising him as her own.

Moses becomes aware of his origins and kills an Egyptian overseer beating a Hebrew slave and flees into Midian to escape punishment. He marries Zipporah, daughter of Midianite priest Jethro, and encounters God in a burning bush who tells him to return to Egypt and lead his people to Canaan, the land He promised to his forbear Abraham.

After Moses leaves Egypt at age 40 he spends another 40 years in Midian before returning to Egypt and fails to convince the Pharaoh to release the Israelites. God smites the Egyptians with ten terrible plagues ending with the death of Egypt's firstborn sons. The Pharaoh reneges on his coerced consent to free the Hebrew slaves and pursues them to the Red Sea where Moses uses his staff to part the Sea, and the Israelites cross on dry ground, but the sea closes down on the pursuing Egyptians, drowning them all. (Exodus 1-14)

The Israelites spend 40 more years wandering toward the Promised Land. They complain about the hardships of desert living and God provides water and manna to eat. Amalek attacks at Rephidim and is defeated in battle. Jethro advices Moses to establish order by putting leaders in charge of their tribes and the appointment of judges for the tribes of Israel. The Israelites reach Mt. Sinai and God gives Moses the Ten Commandments and the Torah laws. If they obey God's laws, they will enter the Promised Land in Canaan. While Moses was on Mt. Sinai for 40 days and nights the people created an idol in the form of a golden calf and God has the Levites kill three thousand people as punishment. (Exodus 32:28)

Moses sends twelve spies ahead to Canaan to scout the land. The spies report that the Israelites cannot defeat the Canaanites who are giants and they do not invade. (Numbers 13:31-33) God declares other than Joshua and Caleb (who were not afraid to invade) no former slave will enter Canaan. A group of Israelites led by Korah, son of Izhar, rebel against Moses and God opens the earth and swallows them. The Israelites come to the oasis of Kadesh Barnea, where Miriam dies and the Israelites remain for most of the forty years.

The Israelites then go to Mount Hor, where Aaron dies. The Israelites complain about lack of bread and water, so God sends a plague of poisonous snakes to afflict them. Moses prays for deliverance and God creates the brazen serpent, and the Israelites who look at it are cured. The Israelites are soon in conflict with various other kingdoms. Some Israelites begin having sexual relations with Moabite women and worshipping Moabite gods so God orders Moses to impale the idolaters and sends a plague, but the full extent of God's wrath is averted when Phinehas impales an Israelite and a Midianite woman having intercourse. (Numbers 25:7-9) God commands the Israelites to destroy the Midianites (genocide). On the banks of the Jordan River Moses addresses the Israelites for a final time and God commissions Joshua to lead the conquest of Canaan. Moses ascends Mount Nebo where he sees the Promised Land and then dies.

The Promised Land of Canaan

Joshua leads the tribes over the Jordan River into Canaan and sends two spies to Jericho who are befriended by Rahab, a Canaanite woman. Because of Rahab's actions the Hebrews can enter Canaan. The Israelites are circumcised at Gibeath-Haaraloth (hill of foreskins), renamed Gilgal in memory. The conquest begins with Jericho followed by Ai (central Canaan). Joshua builds an altar to God at Mount Ebal, renews the Covenant and does a divine land-grant ceremony.

The Israelites go south make an alliance with the Gibeonites and enslave them. God miraculously stops the sun and moon and hurls down large hailstones (Joshua 10:10–14) so the Israelites can defeat an alliance of Amorite kingdoms headed by the Canaanite king of Jerusalem. The enemy kings were hanged on trees. Then northern Canaan is conquered, and the entire land is totally vanquished mostly by military means.

Joshua is *old, advanced (or stricken) in years* after conquering Canaan. (Joshua 13:1) and then had to distribute land as a *covenantal land grant*. God, as king, is issuing each tribe its territory. The *Cities of Refuge* and Levitical cities were attached to the end. In Joshua's farewell speeches (Joshua 23-24) he tells the tribal leaders to obey the Law of Moses. When he meets with people at Shechem he recounts the history of God's formation of the Israelite nation, beginning with *Terah, the father of Abraham and Nahor, who lived beyond the Euphrates River and worshiped other gods*. (Joshua 24:2) The Israelites were told to choose between serving the Lord who had delivered them from Egypt, or the pagan gods of their ancestors and the Amorites. The people chose to serve the Lord.

After Joshua died the rule of Judges began with frequent apostasy, provoking Divine chastening. Urgent appeals to God in times of crisis, moved the Lord to raise up leaders (judges) through whom He defeats foreign oppressors and restores peace. Many of the covenantal promises God had historically made were fulfilled. (Jos 21:43-45) The *stiff necked* people lost sight of their unique identity and attached to Canaanite morals, gods, beliefs, and practices. In the very center of the cycle of the judges, Gideon had to remind Israel that the Lord was their King. There were recurring cycles of disobedience, foreign oppression, cries of distress, and deliverance from God.

The age of Judges without a human king and dismissing the King of the Universe was Israel's failure and it followed directly after the redemptive events that came from Moses and Joshua. The commonly followed dating of ancient events is from 2Ki 6:1 that defines the interval between the Exodus and the fourth year of Solomon's reign to 480 years: ergo the Exodus took place in 1446 BCE and the period of the Judges was between c 1380 and the rise of Israel's first King Saul in c 1050.

The Book of Judges portrays the character of a chaotic age and a large-scale failure with Divine rebuke. The narrative of the Book of Judges focuses on five major judges:

1. Ehud (3:12-30) delivers Israel from oppression from the east;
2. Deborah (4-5) reigns during the time Israel was being overrun by a coalition of Canaanites under Sisera;

3. Gideon, the ideal judge like Moses and his son
    Abimelech (6-9) who was not ideal;
4. Jephthah (10:6-12:7) a social outcast at a time
    when Israel was being threatened by a coalition
    of powers under the Ammon king;
5. Samson (13-16) delivers Israel from oppression
    from the west.

The two Books of Kings presents a history of ancient Israel and Judah from the death of King David to the release of Jehoiachin from imprisonment in Babylon, a period of some 400 years (c 960 – c 560 BCE). In King David's old age, his son Solomon becomes King and builds the First Temple in Jerusalem. The nation is split in two because of Solomon's failure to eradicate idolatry. David's son Rehoboam rules in Judah and the northern kingdom (Israel) has a rapid succession of dynasties that rule poorly and do not follow the Law of Moses. God sends the Assyrians to destroy the northern kingdom. The 14th king of Judah, Hezekiah instituted religious reform with Temple sacrifice and destruction of the idols. God saves the kingdom from an invasion by Assyria. The next king Manasseh reverses the reforms, and God announces that he will destroy Jerusalem because of this apostasy by the king. Manasseh's righteous grandson Josiah reinstitutes the reforms of Hezekiah, but it is too late and God, via the prophetess Huldah, affirms that Jerusalem will to be destroyed after the death of Josiah. In c 740 BCE the Assyrians invaded Israel and Judah resettling the Israeli captives (the Assyrian Exile). The Neo-Assyrian Empire on many occasions forcibly relocated and exiled the Israelis. The Northern Kingdom of Israel was conquered by successive Neo-Assyrian monarchs; Tiglath-Pileser III, Shalmaneser V, Sargon II and his son and successor, Sennacherib. The Neo-Assyrians were responsible for the demise of the northern ten-tribe kingdom. They besieged Jerusalem and the Southern Kingdom but did not conquer it. The forcibly relocated tribes became known as the *Ten Lost Tribes.* (1 Chronicles 5:26 2 Kings 15:29 2 Kings 18:11–12)

According to 2nd Chronicles, Chapter 30, there is evidence that at least some people of the Northern Kingdom of Israel were not exiled. These were invited by king Hezekiah (who may have annexed Judea) to keep the Passover in a feast at Jerusalem with the Judean population. The king sent posts and letters to the people of Israel and Judea saying:

> *Ye children of Israel, turn back unto the LORD, the God of Abraham, Isaac, and Israel, that He may return to the remnant that are escaped out of the*

hand of the kings of Assyria. And be ye not like your fathers and like your brethren who acted treacherously against the LORD, the God of their fathers, so that He delivered them to desolation, as ye see. Now be ye not stiff necked as your fathers were but yield yourselves unto the LORD and enter into His sanctuary which He hath sanctified forever; and serve the LORD your God that His fierce anger may turn away from you.

For if ye turn back unto the LORD, your brethren and your children shall find compassion before them that led them captive, and shall come back into this land; for the LORD your God is gracious and merciful, and will not turn away His face from you if ye return unto Him. (2 Chronicles 30:5–9)

The remnant of the Kingdom of Israel returned home after destroying the Ba'al and Ashera places of Idol worship left in *all Judah and Benjamin, in Ephraim also and Manasseh.* (2 Chronicles 31)

Then in 586 BCE The Neo-Babylonian Empire of King Nebuchadnezzar invades and destroys Jerusalem and the First Temple. The priests, prophets and royal court are led into another captivity and exile (the Babylonian Exile). The dates, numbers of deportations, and numbers of deportees given in the biblical accounts vary. These deportations are dated to 597 BCE for the first, with others dated at 587/586 BCE, and 582/581 BCE respectively.[4]

In 539 the Persian king Cyrus the Great of the Achaemenid Empire conquered Babylon and the exiled Judeans were permitted to return to Judah in 538 BCE led by Prophets Ezra and Nehemiah.[5] Construction of the Second Jerusalem Temple began around 537 BCE according to the Book of Ezra. The last Prophets Haggai, Zechariah, and Malachi in 516 BCE led the completion of the Temple rebuilding. The Babylonian exile return was not a single event but a more gradual process. Many of the deportees or their descendants did not return, becoming the ancestors of the Iraqi Jews. Gedaliah, a native Judahite was the first Babylonian appointed governor of Judah and he encouraged Jews who had fled to return. A surviving member of the royal family assassinated Gedaliah and his Babylonian advisors. The assassination prompted many refugees to seek safety in Egypt. By the end of the 6th century BCE there were significant numbers of Jews in Judah, Babylon, and Egypt; the beginning of numerous Jewish communities living permanently outside Judah in the Jewish Diaspora.[6]

In the Tenach the captivity in Babylon is punishment for idolatry and disobedience to God. During the Babylonian Captivity the current Hebrew alphabet was adopted; the last high-point of prophecy was seen with Ezekiel; the Torah became central to Jewish life; Jews were transformed into an ethno-religious group who could survive without a central Temple; scribes and sages emerged as leaders; people organized in smaller family groups rather than tribes.[7]

Under the Persians and Greeks leadership passed to five successive generations of *zugot* (pairs of) leaders and the religious sects of Pharisees and Sadducees were formed. The Hellenistic period (c 332–110 BCE) in Israel started when Alexander the Great of Macedon defeated the Persians and his Generals after him formed the Seleucid Kingdom. Another Jewish diaspora to Alexandria occurred culminating in the compilation of the Septuagint (Greek Bible translation).

After the death of Alexander altercations between his generals led to the division of his empire among three generals. Antigonus and then Ptolemy inherited Egypt; Seleucus, inherited the Middle East and Mesopotamia. After two centuries of Persian peace in Israel, the Hebrew state found itself caught in the middle of power struggles between two great empires: the Seleucid state to the north and the Ptolemaic state to the south. Judah was conquered and shifted from being a Seleucid vassal state to a Ptolemaic vassal state. Between 319 and 302 BCE, Jerusalem changed hands seven times. The Greeks were more foreign to the Hebrews than any other occupying force. The Greek gods seemed wildly offensive with the human naked form revered and worshipped. The Greek attitude and even preference for homosexuality must have been incomprehensible. Adopting Persian king Cyrus's policies, the Greeks allowed the Jews to run things under the law of Torah and preserve the Jewish religion.

A Jewish revolt was touched off under the Maccabees when the Seleucid king, Antiochus IV, desecrated the Temple in 168 BCE. For a brief time, Judah became an independent state again as the Hasmonaean Kingdom (110–63 BCE). The Greek defeat and rededication of the Temple is celebrated as the Holiday of Chanukah.

During the time of the Greeks and Hasmonaeans, Jews were living in Judah, Mesopotamia, other parts of the Middle East, and Egypt. In the ancient world, it was not possible to become a citizen of a state if you were not born in that state. You were always an Israelite no matter where you lived, and your legal status was "foreigner" or "sojourner". In the *polis* the Greeks allowed foreigners to become citizens. Being able to have citizenship elsewhere was vital to the Jewish dispersion and Jews were allowed and able to thrive in Judah and elsewhere. In Ptolemaic Egypt, the Torah was translated into Greek (Septuagint) and copies were placed in the library at Alexandria and it became the authoritative code of the Jews recognized by Persia and Greece. In 458 BCE, Artaxerxes I of Persia made the Torah *the law of the Judaean king*. The Septuagint made the Hebrew religion a world religion.[8]

The Hasmonean Kingdom of the Maccabees. disintegrated resulting from a civil war between the Hasmonean sons of Salome Alexandra, Hyrcanus II, and Aristobulus II. Pompey conquered and annexed the land and Rome ruled the land of Israel (63 BCE–324 CE). Due to economic hardship and incessant warfare over Israel by the Ptolemaic and Seleucid Empires another Jewish diaspora saw migrations to Rome, Roman Europe, Asia Minor, Babylon, and Alexandria. In Rome, Jewish communities enjoyed privileges and thrived economically, becoming a significant part of the Empire's population.

Julius Caesar conquered Alexandria c 47 BCE and defeated Pompey in c 45 BCE and officially recognized Judaism as a legal religion, a policy followed by the first Roman emperor, Augustus. The Roman Senate declared Herod the Great 'King of the Jews' in c 40 BCE whose offspring formed the Herodian dynasty. Judea proper became the Roman province of Iudaea in 6 CE. The Jews did not have the status of *religio licita* (permitted religion) as this status did not exist in the Roman empire; instead, the regulations were made as a response to individual requests to the emperor. In 30 or 33 CE Jesus of Nazareth, an itinerant Galilee Rabbi was crucified by the Roman prefect of Judaea, Pontius Pilate. During the Roman occupation it is estimated they crucified 100,000 Jews and slaughtered a total of one million.

Tensions between Jews and Rome resulted in several Jewish–Roman wars (66–135 CE). The wars resulted in the destruction of Jerusalem and the Second Temple in 70 CE along with a Jewish Tax which had to be paid for Jews to practice Judaism. In 70 CE the Romans had taken about 100,000 Jews into slavery and captivity and scattered many from Palestine to other locations in the Roman Empire. Jews were exiled from Jerusalem as the fourth and longest Diaspora began. Jews in Cyprus, Cyrene, Egypt, and Mesopotamia revolted against the Roman Empire in 113 CE causing the death of several hundreds of thousands of Romans and Jews. Julius Severus ravaged Judea while defeating the Bar Kokhba revolt of 132–136 CE. 985 villages were destroyed and most of Jewish population of central Judea was essentially wiped out (about 500,000 killed), thousands were sold into slavery, or forced into exile throughout the known world. Banished from Jerusalem which was renamed Aelia Capitolina by Hadrian in 130 CE and Judea was renamed Syria Palestina, to spite the Jews by naming it after their ancient enemies, the Philistines. After 135 CE Jews were forbidden, upon pain of death, from practicing circumcision, reading the Torah, eating unleavened bread at Passover. Temples in and around Jerusalem were dedicated to Roman gods.

Christianity developed from Second Temple Judaism and in 313, Roman Emperors Constantine and Licinius issued the Edict of Milan giving official recognition to Christianity as a legal religion. Constantine the Great moved the Roman capital from Rome to Constantinople ('New Rome' c 330 CE). In 380 CE Christianity became the state church of the Roman Empire. The Christian emperors persecuted their Jewish subjects and restricted their rights. The Jews of all the European cities had lived in Rome the longest, over 2,000 years. Before Rome annexed Judea as a province, the Romans had interacted with Jews from their diasporas when they settled in Rome and Roman provinces since the 6th century BCE.[8]

Diaspora in the Common Era

Judaism moved from a centralized Temple-based religion to the decentralized traditions of the Diaspora. Detailed interpretations of the Torah were composed in the Mishnah and Talmud. The Mishnah commentaries of the *Amoraim* are in the Jerusalem Talmud completed around 400 CE. The Babylonian Talmud was completed around 500 CE. In spite of the failure of the Bar Kokhba revolt and many armed conflicts with consecutive occupiers of the Land some of the most famous and important texts were composed in Israeli cities; the Jerusalem Talmud, the completion of the Mishnah and the system of niqqud (diacritical signs used to represent vowels or distinguish between alternative pronunciations of letters of the Hebrew alphabet). The era of *Tannaim and Amoraim* rabbis organized and debated Jewish oral law. One of the last *Tannaim* was Judah ha Nasi (Judah the Prince) who was believed to have completed the Mishnah in 200 CE. *Tannaim* decisions are contained in the Mishnah, Beraita, Tosefta, and various Mishnah compilations. Rabbi Shimon bar Yochai (Rashbi) composed the Zohar (mystical kabbalah Judaism) in the 2nd century CE while hiding in a cave from the Roman authorities. The Midrash was composed between 100-1000 CE as the genre of rabbinic literature containing early interpretations and commentaries on the Written and Oral Torah (spoken law and sermons). Halakha Midrashim became the running commentary on Tanakh passages, and Aggadah or Haggadah Midrashim became the non-legal portions of the Tenakh explained.

Hillel II created the Hebrew calendar in 359 CE; a lunisolar calendar based on math rather than observation. Until the Hillel II calendar Jews in the diaspora depended on the observational calendar sanctioned by the Sanhedrin which was critical for the proper observance of the Jewish holy days. Religious persecutions of the messengers of the observed calendar convinced Hillel II to authorize a calendar for the present and all future years without the need for observation or messengers. Julian was the only emperor to reject Christianity and allowed the Jews to return to Jerusalem and rebuild the Third Temple, which never happened since

Julian was killed in a 363 CE battle. Empress Eudocia (438 CE) removed the ban on Jews praying at the Temple site but the Jerusalem Christian population were threatened and after a riot erupted the Jews were chased away from the city of Jerusalem. A series of Samaritan insurrections occurred during the 5th and the 6th centuries CE across the Palestina Prima province resulting in nearly annihilating the Samaritan community by the Romans.

Religious conversions to Judaism were forbidden in 200 CE by Roman Emperor Severus and in 306 CE the Synod of Elvira banned marriages, sex, and community contacts between Christians and Jews. In 325 CE the Council of Nicea separated the celebration of Easter and Passover:

> *For it is unbecoming beyond measure that on this holiest of festivals we should follow the customs of the Jews. Henceforth let us have nothing in common with this odious people...We ought not, therefore, to have anything in common with the Jews...our worship follows a...more convenient course...we desire dearest brethren, to separate ourselves from the detestable company of the*

Jews...How, then, could we follow these Jews, who are almost certainly blinded.

Emperor Constantias in 337 CE made the marriage of a Jew to a Christian punishable by death and converting to Judaism in 339 CE became a criminal offense. The Laodicean Synod in 343-381 CE approved Cannon XXXVIII:

It is not lawful [for Christians] to receive unleavened bread from the Jews, nor to be partakers of their impiety.

St. Hilary of Poitiers (367-376 CE) said that Jews were perverse people cursed by God forever and St. Ephroem referred to synagogues as brothels. The Bishop of Milan, responsible for a synagogue burning called it *an act pleasing to God.* St. Cyril, Bishop of Alexandria expelled the Jews from the Egyptian city in 415 CE and St. Augustine wrote:

The true image of the Hebrew is Judas Iscariot, who sells the Lord for silver. The Jew can never understand the Scriptures and forever will bear the guilt for the death of Jesus

St. Jerome created the Vulgate Bible translation (Latin) in 418 CE and wrote about a synagogue:

> *If you call it a brothel, a den of vice,*
> *the Devil's refuge, Satan's fortress,*
> *a place to deprave the soul, an abyss*
> *of every conceivable disaster or*
> *whatever you will, you are still saying*
> *less than it deserves.*

Christian mobs destroyed the synagogues in Antioch, Daphne (near Antioch) and Ravenna (489- 519 CE). The Justinian Code in 528 CE prohibited the building of synagogues, reading the Bible in Hebrew, assembling in public, celebrating Passover before Easter, and testifying against Christians. The Synod of Claremont decreed in 535 CE *that Jews could not hold public office or have authority over Christians.* The 3rd and 4th Councils of Orleans in 538 CE prohibited Jewish-Christian marriage and conversion to Judaism. The Bishop of Uzes in France expelled Jews from his diocese in 561 CE and in 612 CE Jews were not allowed to own land, be farmers, or enter certain trades. In Spain Jews could either leave in exile or convert to Christianity. Jews over the age of six were taken from their parents and given a Christian education (613 CE). Christians were forbidden to live in the homes of Jews in 1050 CE by the

Synod of Narbonne. Pope Gregory VII decreed that Jews could not hold office or be superiors to Christians in 1078 CE and Jews were forced to pay church taxes via the Synod of Gerona the same year.

The Jews allied with the Persians who invaded Palestina Prima in 614 CE were given Jerusalem to govern; within three weeks it fell into anarchy with Christians revolting. Around 625 CE the Persian forces withdrew, and the Jews surrendered to the Byzantines, but were massacred by Christian radicals in 629 CE, with the survivors fleeing to Egypt. During the Byzantine–Sasanian War of 602–628 CE many Jews sided against the Eastern Roman Empire and assisted the invading Persian Sassanids in conquering all of Roman Egypt and Syria. Additional anti-Jewish measures were enacted throughout the Eastern Roman realm because of helping the Persian Sassanids.[9]

In 637 CE the Muslim Arab armies under Umar ibn al-Khattab completed the conquest of Akko and took control of the Byzantine (Eastern Roman Empire) region. Jewish communities existed in the Byzantine Empire from the foundation of Constantinople in 330 CE to the Ottoman conquest of the city in 1453 CE. Jewish centers and the status of the Jews underwent drastic changes in the Byzantine Empire. From Constantine to the Iconoclastic Period (330 to 720 CE) Jews were located in the eastern Mediterranean region (present-day Greece, Asia Minor, Constantinople, Syria, Erez Israel, and Egypt). The attitude of the rulers and society, the methods employed by the Church, and the language of official documents and legislation all combined to humiliate the Jews, narrow Jewish society, religion, and opportunities open to Jews. Emperor Constantine described the Jewish religion as *baleful* and threatened them with capital punishment for interfering with converts to Christianity. It became a crime to become Jewish. Jews who circumcised their slaves forfeited the slaves' ownership. (Cod. Theod. 16:8 (4, 1, 5)) Marriage between Jews and Christians was forbidden. An abortive revolt in Israel against the provincial commander Gallus was suppressed in 351 CE.

Emperor Theodosius I revived missionary activity and prohibited Jewish parents from disinheriting children who had apostatized to Christianity. A synagogue in Callinicum (Mesopotamia) in 388 CE was burned and the bishop of Milan, Ambrose compelled the Emperor not to punish the perpetrators. The temporary Jewish expulsion from Alexandria by the patriarch Cyril in 415 CE was a victory for the Church and authorities who had stirred up Jewish hatred. The code of Theodosius II (438 CE) summed up former anti-Jewish legislation: Jews could not own slaves; could not build new synagogues; could not hold public office; could not try cases between a Jew and a non-Jew; Intermarriage was a capital offence; Conversion to Judaism was a capital offence; The Sanhedrin was abolished; civil rights were restricted; religious privileges were threatened; use of Hebrew in worship was forbidden. Disobeying included corporal penalties, exile, and loss of property.

Certain Purim celebrations were forbidden. In the fourth century CE there developed vitriolic anti-Jewish polemic literature. Writers and preachers shared their acrimony toward, and vilification of, the Jews and Judaism. Pulpit sermons by John Chrysostom in Antioch (387 CE) ascribed every imaginable evil to the Jews. His sermons had titles such as *Against the Jews and On the Statues, Homily 17,* in which he preaches against the *Jewish sickness.* Such heated language contributed to a climate of Christian distrust and hate toward the large Jewish settlements, such as those in Antioch and Constantinople. The spoken and written venom toward Jews to a large degree lies at the root of medieval Jew-hatred that spread beyond the boundaries of the Byzantine Empire and its culture.

The sixth century CE reign of Justinian I made attitudes and treatment of the Jews worse. The Jewish-Arab kingdom of Himyar in southern Arabia was destroyed, instigated by the authorities. Justinian's *novella* 146 in 553 CE dictated Jewish divine worship and forbade the use of the *deuterosis* (Mishnah) for understanding the Torah; he mandated which biblical translation (Targum in the Aramaic language) could be used. Anti-Jewish riots and forced conversions were common in the second half of the sixth and first half of the seventh centuries CE. Jews (most notable Benjamin of Tiberias) allied themselves with the Persians during their capture of Jerusalem and on its recapture (629 CE) and under Emperor Heraclius the Jews underwent a series of vengeful massacres. A council presided over by Emperor Justinian II in 692 CE prohibited Jews and Christians from bathing together in public places, and Christians from consulting Jewish physicians.

The Jews gradually withdrew from or were forced out of civic life. Jewish communal life and local leadership by the elders was well established. Birth, wealth, and scholarship were the major factors in attaining leadership positions. Economically the Jews were only gradually ousted from their professions and positions of wealth, and from their places of residence in the cities. Many engaged in overland and maritime commerce. Dyeing became a major Jewish industry through 1400 CE. The center of Jewish culture was in Israel as the main source of liturgical poetry.

From 720 through 1204 CE Jews continued to live in the major cities throughout the Empire. Iconoclasts were branded in sermons and tales circulated they were Jews. The final restoration of icon worship in 843 CE was accompanied by renewed violent anti-Jewish manifestations. Basil I decreed the forcible conversion of his Jewish subjects in 873–74 CE which was rescinded by Leo VI. In 943 CE Romanus I Lecapenus made another attempt at forcible conversion. Many Jews fled their homes to avoid these persecutions. In 11th and 12th centuries CE the Byzantine Jews lived under a regime of absolute humiliation although somewhat assured of relative safety for their lives and property. Jewish occupations included agriculture, silk weaving, and cloth dyeing industries. Two elders led smaller communities and five elders led larger communities.

The Christian Crusades (1096–1272 CE) to avenge the death of Jesus was encouraged. Although the prime goal of the crusades was to liberate Jerusalem from the Muslims, Jews were a second target. Crusaders traveling to Holy Land in the First Crusade massacred Jews residing in their midst beginning at Rouen communities in Rhine Valley (12,000 Jews were slaughtered). This behavior continued for eight additional crusades until the 9th in 1272 CE. These massacres were the first in a sequence of anti-Semitic events which culminated in the Holocaust. The Crusaders in 1099 CE forced the Jews of Jerusalem into a central synagogue and set it on fire and forced all escapees back into the burning building. The Fourth Crusade (1204 CE) burned and pillaged the Jewish quarter of Constantinople. Many Venetian Jews engaged in tanning, and the majority apparently were wealthy. In the parts of Greece and the Balkans, various Greek rulers issued Jewish proscriptions at times (1214 to 1230 CE in Epirus and Salonika and 1222-1254 CE in Nicea).[10]

Jews were expelled and exiled in large numbers from 1100 to 1500 CE:

- from France, Silesia, Crimea, and Flanders (now part of Belgium) in the 1100s;

- from Wales and England (the Crown took all Jewish possessions and burned most of their homes) in the 1200s;

- From France (three times with only the clothes they wore and one day of food), Germany, Crimea, Hungary (two times) in the 1300s;

- from Portugal, Spain, Austria, Sardinia, Sicily, Provence, Silesia, Lithuania (two times) in 1400s;

- from Tunis, Naples, Papal States (two times), Germany (two times), Genoa, Venice, Holland in the 1500s.

In 1130 CE some London Jews were blamed for killing a sick man and were required to pay 1 million marks as compensation. The expelled and exiled Jews resettled in Netherlands, Poland, Ottoman Empire, Egypt, and Maghreb.

The Fourth Lateran Council in 1215 CE approved canon laws requiring that *Jews and Muslims shall wear a special dress.* They also had to wear a badge in the form of a ring to be easily distinguished and the practice later spread to other countries; e.g., The Synod of Narbonne in 1227 CE required Jews to wear an oval badge and in 1259 CE a synod of the Mainz archdiocese ordered Jews to wear yellow badges. In 1267 CE the Synod of Vienna ordered Jews to wear horned hats and Thomas Aquinas said that Jews should live in perpetual servitude. In 1434 CE:

Jewish men in Augsburg had to sew yellow buttons to their clothes. Across Europe, Jews were forced to wear a long undergarment, an overcoat with a yellow patch, bells, and tall pointed yellow hats with a large button on them.

A Roman Catholic Papal bull, *Cum nimis absurdum* in 1555 CE required Jews to wear badges, and live in ghettos under dreadful conditions. Women had to wear a yellow veil or scarf; men had to wear a piece of yellow cloth on their hat. In the 1930s Adolf Hitler changed the yellow badges, patches, and hats to a yellow Star of David.

The Spanish inquisition began in 1229 CE and in 1236: Pope Gregory ordered church leaders in England, France, Portugal, and Spain to confiscate Jewish books on the first Saturday of Lent. Pope Innocent IV authorized the Inquisitors to use torture in 1252 CE.

Duke Henry III of Brabant, Belgium in 1261 CE stated in his will that:

> *Jews...must be expelled from Brabant and totally annihilated so that not a single one remains, except those who are willing to trade, like all other tradesmen, without moneylending and usury.*

Jews were persecuted in Austria, Bavaria, and Franconia in 1298 CE. Over 100,000 were killed within six months and 140 Jewish communities were destroyed. In the Shepherd Crusade 40,000 French shepherds went to Palestine and destroyed 140 Jewish communities on their way in 1320 CE. One year later in Guienne, France 5,000 Jews were burned alive at the stake being accused of inciting criminals to poison wells. Starting in 1347 the Black Plague, the worst pandemic in human history killed between 25-200 million people. Due to sanitary and dietary laws a smaller percentage of Jews caught the disease. Rumors spread that the payback to Satan for protecting Jews was poisoning Christian wells. Jews were tortured, murdered, and burned by tens of thousands.

In 1354 CE 12,000 Jews were executed in Toledo, Spain and in 1391 CE Jewish persecutions began in Seville and in 70 other Jewish communities throughout Spain. An epidemic of wild raving occurred in the lower Rhine region (Germany) for St. John's Day in 1374. Exorcisms and pilgrimages were tried but failed. The revelers believed that God was angry because of excessive tolerance towards the Jews. Jews were plundered, tortured, and murdered by tens of thousands until the epidemic burned itself out two centuries later (late 16th century).

In 1431 CE the Council of Basel

> *forbade Jews to go to universities, prohibited them from acting as agents in the conclusion of contracts between Christians, and required that they attend church sermons.*

The Franciscan monk, Capistrano in 1453 CE persuaded the King of Poland to terminate all Jewish civil rights. Due to heavy persecution in the 14th century many Jews converted to Christianity. In 1478 CE the Spanish Inquisition set out to detect insincere conversions. Laws prohibited the descendants of Jews or Muslims from attending university, joining religious orders, holding public office, or entering many professions. In 1492 CE (the year of Columbus' discovery of the new world) Jews were given the choice of being baptized or banishment. 300,000 left Spain without any money and many migrated to Turkey where there was more Muslim tolerance. Others converted and often practiced Judaism secretly. Similarly, Portugal offered the same option, conversion, or banishment...20,000 left the country. Shortly thereafter (1516 CE) the Republic of Venice Governor created the first European Ghetto, *Ghetto Novo* in the South Girolamo parish. Adolf Hitler created Jewish Ghettos in the 1930's.

Martin Luther wrote and preached Jewish hatred after Jews did not convert to Christianity. He expressed this hatred in his letters to Rev. Spalatin in 1514 CE:

> *I have come to the conclusion that the Jews will always curse and blaspheme God and his King Christ, as all the prophets have predicted....For they are thus given over by the wrath of God to reprobation, that they may become incorrigible, as Ecclesiastes says, for everyone who is incorrigible is rendered worse rather than better by correction.*

In 1543, he wrote *On the Jews and their lies, On Shem Hamphoras:*

> *...eject them forever from this country. For, as we have heard, God's anger with them is so intense that*

gentle mercy will only tend to make them worse and worse, while sharp mercy will reform them but little. Therefore, in any case, away with them! What then shall we Christians do with this damned, rejected race of Jews?

First, their synagogues or churches should be set on fire,

Secondly, their homes should likewise be broken down and destroyed... They ought to be put under one roof or in a stable, like Gypsies.

Thirdly, they should be deprived of their prayer books and Talmuds in which such idolatry, lies, cursing and blasphemy are taught.

Fourthly, their rabbis must be forbidden under threat of death to teach any more...

Fifthly, passport and traveling privileges should be absolutely forbidden to the Jews...

Sixthly, they ought to be stopped from usury. All their cash and valuables of silver and gold ought to be taken from them and put aside for safe keeping...

Seventhly, let the young and strong Jews and Jewesses be given the flail, the axe, the hoe, the spade, the distaff, and spindle and let them earn their bread by the sweat of their noses as in enjoined upon Adam's children...

To sum up, dear princes and nobles who have Jews in your domains, if this advice of mine does not suit you, then find a better one so that you and we may all be free of this insufferable devilish burden - the Jews.

Chmielnicki Bogdan led an uprising against Polish rule in the Ukraine (1648-1649 CE). Bogdan's secondary goal was the extermination of Jews. Mass slaughters are estimated at 100,000 with 300 communities destroyed.

Leadership in medicine by the 10th century was provided largely by Jewish and Muslim scholars. Jews were largely responsible for founding the medical Schools at Salerno and Montpellier in the 10th century. The Christian Church during the Middle Ages restricted Medicine in Europe as the church taught that it was irreligious to seek a natural cure from a physician when one could obtain supernatural help from a priest. Medical schools were criticized because they taught that diseases and disorders came from natural means and not from the evil of Satan. Pope Eugene IV, Nicholas V and Calixtus III forbade Christians from using the services of a Jewish physician along with:

- The Trullanean Council in the 8th century;

- Béziers Council & Alby Council in the 13th century;

- Avignon council & Salamanca Council in the 14th century;

- The Synod of Bamberg in the 15th century;

- The Council of Avignon in the 16th century;

- When the city of Hall in Würtemberg, Germany in the 17th century granted some privileges to a Jewish physician *on account of his admirable experience and skill.* The clergy of Hall complained that: *It was better to die with Christ than to be cured by a Jew doctor aided by the devil.*

In the late Middle Ages, Jews were about 1% of Europe's population and constituted about 50% of its physicians. The chief court physicians of the rulers and Popes of Europe were Jews or crypto-Jews:

- Frederick III of the Holy Roman Empire;
- Ferdinand and Isabella of Spain;
- Elizabeth I of England;
- Louis XIV of France;
- Catherine de Medici and Catherine the Great of Russia;
- Pope Martin IV, Pope Nicholas IV, Pope Boniface VIII, Pope Alexander VI, Pope Julius II, Pope Leo X, Pope Clement VII, Pope Paul III, Pope Gregory XV, Pope Urban VIII, and Pope Innocent X.

Prior to 1800 CE persecution was religiously based and called anti-Judaism. After 1800 it became racial and was called anti-Semitism making Jew haters sound less vulgar. The term antisemitism was first used in a pamphlet by Wilhelm Marr called *Jewry's Victory over Teutonism* in 1873 CE. Abbe Barruel, a French Jesuit Priest wrote a treatise in 1806 CE blaming the Masons, then the Jews for the French Revolution. This led to the belief later in the 19th century of an international Jewish conspiracy in Germany, Poland, and other European countries. Pope Pius IX (1846-1878 CE) restored all previous restrictions against Jews within the Vatican state, and they were confined to Rome's ghetto; the last one in Europe until the Nazi era. In 2000 CE Pope John Paul II beatified Pope Pius IX; the last step before sainthood. Radicals assassinated Alexander II of Russia and in 1883 CE the Jews were blamed followed by about 200 pogroms (often supported and organized by the government). Pogrom is Russian for devastation or riot when Jewish individuals, shops, homes, and businesses are destroyed. Thousands became homeless and impoverished. The Tsarist government organized an anti-Jewish pogrom in Kishinev, Moldova, Russia in 1903 CE. Relatives murdered a Christian child and a young Christian woman committed suicide at a Jewish Hospital. Jews were blamed and violence was assured. The 5,000 town soldiers did nothing as there were: 49 dead and 500 wounded Jews; 700 homes looted and destroyed; 600 businesses and shops looted; and 2,000 families homeless. In 1942 CE almost 18,000 Russian inhabitants of the Minsk ghetto in what is now Belarus were exterminated. Additionally, 5,000 to 15,000 had been massacred in earlier Minsk pogroms. There were numerous pogroms during World War II. Even after World War II ended anti-Semitic pogroms continued, particularly in Poland, with the deaths of many Jews.

Anti-Semitic parties won sixteen seats in the German Reichstag in 1893 CE and a year later in France Captain Alfred Dreyfus, on the French general staff, was sentenced to life in prison for treason on forged papers by anti-Semitic officers. The church, the government, and the army united to suppress the truth. The Dreyfus sentence motivated Journalist Theodor Herzl to write *The Jewish State: A Modern Solution to the Jewish Question* in 1896 CE. The Zionist movement was born for a Jewish Homeland.

Another long remembered and still utilized anti-Semitic event occurred in 1905 CE: During Czar Nicholas II reign the Russian secret police (Okhrana) converted an earlier anti-Semitic novel into a document called the *Protocols of the Elders of Zion* published privately in 1897 CE. A Russian Orthodox priest, Sergius Nilus, published them publicly in 1905 CE. It was promoted as the record of *secret rabbinical conferences whose aim was to subjugate and exterminate the Christians*. The Okhrana used the *Protocols* as propaganda and reason to massacre the Jews known as the Czarist Pogroms of 1905. By 1915 CE 600,000 Russian Jews were forcibly moved from the western borders to the interior. About 100,000 died of exposure or starvation. Two years later in the civil war following the Bolshevik Revolution of 1917, the reactionary White Armies made extensive use of the *Protocols* to incite widespread slaughters of Jews. Two hundred thousand Jews were murdered in the Ukraine alone. *Yevsektsiya* was_the Jewish section of the Bolshevik Party that did Lenin's bidding with zeal until the communist regime rounded them up, too. The *Protocols* reached England and the United States in 1920 CE and even though exposed as a forgery they were widely circulated. Henry Ford sponsored a study of international activities of Jews that led to a series of anti-Semitic articles in the *Dearborn Independent*, then published in a book, *The International Jew*.

The defeat of Germany in World War I and its economic difficulties were blamed on the Jewish influence. Hitler had published *Mein Kampf* in 1925 CE and wrote:

> *Today I believe that I am acting in*
> *accordance with the will of the*
> *ALMIGHTY Creator by defending myself*
> *against the Jew, I am fighting*
> *for the work of the Lord.*

The Nazis used the *Protocols* to whip up public hatred and in the 1930's widespread pogroms occurred in Greece, Hungary, Mexico, Poland, Rumania, and the USSR. Many conservative American clergy frequently attacked Jews on their radio programs. Reverend Fr. Charles E Coughlin was one of the best known. His radio audiences heard him rail against Jews and the economy and defend Hitler's treatment of them as justified in the fight against communism. North American Jewish discrimination was widespread in the 1930s as many universities established quotas limiting the number of Jewish students. Jews were commonly barred from country clubs, prestigious neighborhoods, local service clubs, etc.

From 1933 through 1945 the Nazis enacted increasingly horrific laws against the Jews. They started by banning them from civil service, legal professions, and universities. They were not allowed to teach in school and could not be editors of newspapers. Then they were no longer considered citizens (Nuremberg Laws). Cardinal Hloud of Poland urged Catholics to boycott Jewish businesses. Kristallnacht (night of broken glass) killed 91 and injured hundreds of Jews, burned 177 synagogues, and looted 7,500 Jewish stores. The Vichy government of France collaborated by freezing about 80,000

Jewish bank accounts and deporting about 76,000 Jews to Nazi death camps. The *Shoah* (Holocaust) was the *Final Solution to the Jewish Question* by the systematic extermination of Jews. Approximately 6 million Jews (1.5 million of them children), and 400 thousand Roma (Gypsies) were slaughtered.

Since the Romans destroyed the Second Temple almost 2,000 years ago and sent the Jews in another Diaspora there were endless horrors: Persecution, passion plays at Easter portraying the Jewish Christ killers, pogroms (organized massacres), forced conversions, synagogue burnings, mass murders, blood baths, scapegoats, poisoning wells accusations, host desecrations accusations (malicious use of sacred bread), blood libels (accusing Jews of using Christian blood to make matza), expulsions, stake burnings, enslavements, ghettos, property confiscation, and outlawing Judaism, Jews, and Jewish communities. Nevertheless, miracles were plentiful. During the Byzantine Empire Geonic Academies (*Geonim* means splendor or geniuses) became the center for Jewish scholarship and the development of Jewish law in Babylonia from roughly c 500 CE to 1038 CE. The *Savoraim* (reasoners) were sages of *beth midrash* (Torah study places) in Babylon from the end of the era of the *Amoraim*

(5th century) until the beginning of the era of the *Geonim* in c 650 CE. The yeshivot of Babylonia served the same function as the Sanhedrin, i.e., as the council of Jewish religious authorities.

The Arab Islamic Empire under Caliph Omar conquered Jerusalem, Mesopotamia, Syria, Palestine and Egypt beginning the Islamic Period (638–1099 CE). After 500 years Jews were again permitted in Jerusalem and were able to hold numerous jobs: assayers of coins; the dyers; the tanners; the bankers; and service in government.

There was a Jewish Golden Age in early Muslim Spain (711–1100 CE). Jews generally were accepted in society and Jewish religious, cultural, and economic life blossomed: in sciences (botany, geography, medicine, mathematics); poetry; philosophy; commerce and industry; trading in silk and slaves; translating Arabic texts to the Romance languages, as well as translating Greek and Hebrew texts into Arabic. Numerous *piyutim* (liturgical poems recited or chanted) and *midrashim* (biblical exegesis) were recorded in Palestine during the Crusades. Moses Maimonides (Rambam 1135-1204 CE) was a Spanish philosopher, astronomer, physician, polymath in both Judaism and Islam and the cornerstone of Jewish scholarship. He composed the *Mishneh Torah and The Guide for the Perplexed* among many other works. *In The Mishnah Torah* he formulated thirteen principles of faith as required beliefs of Judaism:

1. *The existence of God.*
2. *God's unity and indivisibility into elements.*
3. *God's spirituality and incorporeality.*
4. *God's eternity.*
5. *God alone should be the object of worship.*
6. *Revelation through God's prophets.*
7. *The preeminence of Moses among the prophets.*
8. *The Torah that we have today is the one dictated to Moses by God.*
9. *The Torah given by Moses will not be replaced and that nothing may be added or removed from it.*
10. *God's awareness of all human actions and thoughts.*
11. *Reward of good and punishment of evil.*
12. *The coming of the Jewish Messiah.*
13. *The resurrection of the dead.*

During the numerous exiles and diasporas Jews were protected by other kings, princes, and bishops, because of the crucial services they provided in three areas: finance, administration, and medicine. Christian scholars interested in the Bible would consult with Talmudic rabbis. Court Jews were bankers or businessmen lending money and handling finances of some of the Christian noble houses (Jewish bailiff and *Shtadlan*). They gained social privileges, including up to noble status for themselves, and could live outside the Jewish ghettos. Port Jews were involved in the seafaring and maritime economies, especially in the 17th and 18th centuries. They arrived as refugees from the Inquisition and the expulsion of Jews from Iberia; they could settle in port cities as merchants were interested in their expertise. During the Ottoman period (1300–1600 CE), Jews and most other communities prospered. Compared to others they were the predominant power in commerce and trade as well in diplomacy and other high offices. Turkey was a safe haven for Jews fleeing persecution. In Poland-Lithuania from the 13th to the 17th century Jews enjoyed relative prosperity and freedom. The most prosperous period for Polish Jews was during reign of Zygmunt I (1506–1548 CE) and his son Zygmunt II (1548–1572 CE); the *Qahal* or autonomous Jewish community was established. Polish monarchy appointed Rabbi Jacob Polak, the official Rabbi of Poland in 1503 CE, marking the emergence of the Chief Rabbinate which eventually was given permission to choose their own Chief Rabbi holding power over law and finance, appointing judges, and other officials. Moses Isserles known as the ReMa (1520–1572

CE), an eminent Talmudist of the 16th century, established his yeshiva in Kraków. He was a renowned Talmudic and legal scholar and learned in Kabbalah, history, astronomy, and philosophy. During the 16th and 17th century Poland had the largest Jewish population in Europe and *Yeshivot* were established, under the direction of the rabbis, in the more prominent communities. During this time in Safed, Israel Joseph Karo wrote the Code of Jewish Law - *Shulchan Aruch* (Set Table) in 1563 CE which is the most widely accepted compilation of Jewish law ever written.

During the European Renaissance and Enlightenment (18th century) the Haskalah movement campaigning for European integration gave birth to Reform and Conservative movements and the seeds of Zionism. Hasidic Judaism also began by Rabbi Israel Baal Shem Tov during this time. There were numerous miracle workers in the 17th and 18th centuries CE some of which culminated into Messianic movements. Sabbatai Zevi (1626-1676 CE) and Jacob Frank (1726-1791 CE) who had 500,000 followers mostly in Poland and Eastern Europe.

Manasseh ben Israel wrote in *The Hope of Israel before* appealing to Oliver Cromwell to readmit the Jews (expelled in 1290 CE) and it summarizes the hatred and respect for Jewish survival in all of Europe:

> *Hence it may be seen that God hath not left us; for if one persecutes us, another receives us civilly and courteously; and if this prince treats us ill, another treats us well; if one banisheth us out of his country, another invites us with a thousand privileges ... and do we not see that those Republiques do flourish and much increase in trade who admit the Israelites?"* But it was not for their economic prowess alone that the Jews were valued, it was for a whole host of skills, not the least of which was their expertise in the medical arts.

Because of the Dreyfus Trial, state-sponsored Russian pogroms, and the influence of Theodor Herzl millions of Jews arrived in the United States, Argentina, and Uruguay (1890-1924 CE) mostly from Russia and Eastern Europe. The majority raised families and had prosperous successful careers for themselves and their families.[10]

The Nation of Israel is Born

After the nation of Israel was established, anti-Semitism changed from religious to racist to Zionism. The Israelis were involved with many miracles. They defeated the Arab nations in the 1949 war. They prevailed in the Six-Day War in 1967, the 1973 Yom Kippur War, as well as nearly constant series of ongoing conflicts.

After the Israeli declaration of independence on May 14, 1948, another miracle occurred. Seven Arab nations attacked the newborn State to *push the Jews into the sea.* Outnumbered 100 to 1, Israel repelled the invaders and acquired more Palestinian land than was granted in the UN partition plan. Yigael Yadin, Israel's commander of operations in that war, had a terse explanation of Israel's victory. *It was a miracle*!

During the 1948 war of independence there were other Jewish miracles. The oldest Israeli kibbutz Degania (established in 1910) was attacked by 200 armored Syrian vehicles, including 45 tanks. The only heavy weapons available in Israel were four howitzers used by the French army in the Franco-Prussian War of 1870. Two of the howitzers were dismantled and rushed to Degania. The Commander Lieutenant Colonel Moshe Dayan, had them reassembled before the first Syrian tanks rumbled passed Degania's perimeter. The Israelis scored a hit on the advance tank. The Syrians would have continued the attack had they known that these two obsolete howitzers represented half of Israel's field gun arsenal. Instead, the armored vehicles retreated from the fight and did not return.

Near the Sea of Galilee in Safed 1,000 Arabs were being held off by a small unit of Israeli defenders. During a sudden tropical storm, the Israelis poured their remaining gasoline into 50 empty drums, set them afire, and rolled them down the hill. As the barrels bounced off rocks on the hill it created loud rumbling in addition to the tropical storms rumbling, and the Davidka artillery that was ineffective but extremely loud. The bewildered Arabs imagined some sort of secret weapon was being used and fled, not to return.

The Egyptians were harassing Israeli settlements in the Negev while other columns were moving north. Commander Yigael Yadin used the Bible for strategy. He used a road forgotten for centuries, which ran almost directly to Mushrafa, the Egyptians' central garrison. Bulldozers cleared the road and armored vehicles, jeeps and supply trucks sped at night along the ancient road and conquered the surprised Egyptians destroying their defense system. The war ended 14 days later.

In Judges 7:17-22 Gideon used tactics to defeat the Midianites. He gave each soldier a trumpet (*shofar*) and a clay jar with a torch inside. Divided into three companies, Gideon and his 300 men marched on the enemy camp. He instructed them to blow the trumpet, give a battle cry and light torches, simulating an attack by a large force. As they did so, the Midianite army fled. To liberate the airport at Lydda in the 1948 war the tactics of Gideon were employed. Seven thousand Arab troops were ready to attack the Lydda Airport. Sixteen Israelis dressed as Arabs infiltrated into the city of Lydda. Like Gideon's band of 300 they made such a commotion during the night that the Arabs, totally confused, fired upon each other. Finally, the majority fled back across the border.

The Syrian Army had regrouped east of the Galilee. A Jewish column of 24 homemade armored trucks and cars took the wrong road crossing into Lebanon on the way to relieve a besieged Kibbutz. The column ran into a column of supplies for the Syrian Army in Galilee (many trucks loaded with ammunition, a string of light artillery and 20 new armored cars). The Israelis fired and exploded a gasoline tanker and a truck loaded with grenades. The Syrians abandoned their cargo. The Israelis drove the captured supply train back into Galilee and reached the beleaguered Kibbutz. The Arab besiegers heard rumors that the Jewish army had invaded Lebanon and they fled from Israel.

In the Battle of Mishmar HaEmek, the Israelis were outnumbered 10:3 and held off 1,000 Arab troops by going on the offensive. They took the Arab villages surrounding the kibbutz which led to the Arab Liberation Army's retreat and was the last significant stand of the Arab Liberation Front in the Israeli War of Independence.

The Battle for Katamon the Israelis captured the monastery used as the Arab forces' base, but the Arabs counter attacked as the Israelis were low on supplies with many injuries. The wounded who could not escape were put in a room rigged with explosives. The Iraqi forces also had many casualties and were out of ammunition, so they retreated and soon after Israeli reinforcements arrived. The victory was miraculous as was the survival of the platoon commander (Raful) after being shot in the head he was back in action 30 minutes later.

Ira Rappaport's platoon was surrounded by hundreds of Jordanians with only 25 bullets left in the battle for Mount Zion. Instead of being overrun and killed the Jordanians dropped their weapons and ran away screaming *Abraham*! Rappaport learned years later from a former Jordanian soldier fighting that day. The soldiers all witnessed a vision of Abraham defending the Israelis in the sky above them and had no choice but to drop their weapons and leave.

The victory of the 1948 War was a big miracle composed of a series of little miracles. Over 2500 years ago the prophet Isaiah made a remarkable prophecy concerning Israel regathered back in her land.

> *They that war against thee shall be*
> *as nothing and as a thing of nought...*
> *for I will help thee.* (41:12,13).

Post 1948 the miracles continued. Trees, fruits, and vegetables grow on sandy wastes and malaria swamps. New industries circle many historic cities. Highways and pipelines have been built as never before. Prime Minister David Ben Gurion (Israel's first) knew the Bible, Israeli history, and its land. He dispatched engineers, horticulturists, botanists, and other specialists to rebuild and ensure a successful future for Jews all over the world.

Following Bible clues, copper and iron mines were established. One mining engineer, Abraham Dor observed that at the richest veins of copper —*we come upon the slag and furnaces of ancient Israel. We often get the feeling that someone has just left*. Deuteronomy 8:7-9 was often framed on the walls of mining offices:

> *For the Lord thy God bringeth thee into a good land; a land whose stones are iron and out of whose hills thou mayest dig copper.*

Barren land transformed to the fertility of ancient Israel is a miracle predicted in Scripture. (Amos 9:14-15; Ezek. 36:34-35) It was long assumed that most of Palestine was wasteland, irreclaimable for agriculture. But archaeologists discovered the presence of more than 70 ancient settlement sites in one 65-mile stretch of the Jordan Valley alone, each with its own well for water. Lot, over 3,000 years ago, was not exaggerating when he *lifted his eyes, and he saw all the plain of Jordan, that it was well watered everywhere, even as the garden of the Lord.* (Gen.13:10)

From Dan to Beersheba agricultural settlements had risen beside ancient sites and concrete pumping stations were built over ancient springs or wells. Residents on Beersheba's outskirts receive water from a well from the time of Patriarch Abraham. An arid country like Israel needs forests and trees that have been planted every year since 1948. The forests are named in honor of leaders and friends of the State. The Bible helps Israelis to decide on the kind of trees to plant and where to plant them. The Book of Joshua provided where to build the *Forest of Martyrs.* A forest had existed successfully during the time of Joshua so knowing where the trees would flourish made that area the location for the *Forest of Martyrs.* Abraham put a tamarisk tree in the soil of Beersheba; following his lead Israel planted two million tamarisks in the same area. The tamarisk was found to be one of the few trees that thrives in the south where yearly rainfall is less than six inches. How did Abraham have such knowledge thousands of years before the sciences of Horticulture and Botany?

Jews from the four points of the compass heard the call to come home. (Isa. 43:5,6) Israel's Declaration of Independence stated that Israel *will be open to the immigration of Jews from all countries of their dispersion.* Operation Magic Carpet began in 1949 and 49,000 endangered Yemenite Jews, and some from countries including Saudi Arabia, were airlifted to Israel in a secret operation involving 380 flights by British and American transport planes taking off from Aden. Israel's population increased from 650,000 in 1948 to nearly 6,000,000 in 1998. The miracle of absorption continues.[14]

Ezekiel 38:12,13 predicted that Israel would become an economic envy of the nations. The immigration of Russian Jews has created an explosion in both hi-tech developments and the number of contracts Israeli hi-tech companies have signed with manufacturers worldwide. The New York Stock Exchange lists more hi-tech companies from Israel than any other nation. Israeli Prime Minister Netanyahu said:

> *The failure of Soviet communism to capitalize on the outstanding R & D skills of the Russian Jews was a stroke of good fortune for Israel. We now have the highest per capita of scientists in the world. This has*

put Israel on the cutting edge of technology.[13]

One of the lost tribes (Ethiopian Falashas) were found starving and abused in the Sudan.

From beyond the rivers of Ethiopia my suppliants, even the daughter of my dispersed, shall bring mine offering. (Zephaniah 3:10)

In Operation Moses in 1991 CE the Falasha in Sudan were airlifted to Israel by the tens of thousands and in later years airlifted from Ethiopia where they had long been persecuted for their beliefs. There are now about 100,000 Falasha Jews in Israel. Israel became the only nation in recorded history not to enslave and export black Africans but to take them out by the tens of thousands for freedom and a better life in their Promised Land.

In the 1967 Six-Day-War Egypt began moving large numbers and heavy artillery to the Sinai desert and closed the Straits of Tiran to Israeli ships and any ship bringing military equipment to Israel. Israel's success was miraculous. Two hundred Israeli Air Force planes were heading towards Egyptian air bases detected by Jordanian radar who sent the message to Egypt as *Inab* (a code for war). Miraculously the Egyptian coding frequencies were changed the previous day unknown to Jordan. Egypt's anti-aircraft missiles were enough to destroy all Israeli planes. Miraculously, no order was given to launch any of those missiles as Israel took down half the Egyptian air force (204 planes) that were preparing to attack Israel. This was the first battle of the Six Day War.

The Battle of Ammunition Hill in 1967 was furious as Israel used paratroopers to minimize civilian casualties but had incorrect intelligence and sent one third of the troops needed. Israel miraculously won this battle in an incredible four hours! Ammunition Hill became a national memorial site.

To win the Six Day War, Israel needed to retake the Egyptians' heavily fortified Kusseima outpost. There were massive explosions as the Israeli forces drew near as the Egyptians had destroyed their equipment and abandoned the base, for no apparent reason! The Egyptians were hastily abandoning many of their outposts and their supplies along with them. One Egyptian soldier said they saw a gigantic hand come out of the sky when they neared the Israeli border and fled terrified of this supernatural event.

On 6-7-1967 after days of violent battles in Jerusalem, Jordanian firing stopped. The city was empty save for the Jordanian equipment left behind. The Israeli forces entered East Jerusalem, and took the Temple Mount, reaching the Western Wall without even firing a single shot. On 6-8-1967 for the first time in 2,000 years Israel not only had the land, but had her holiest city, Jerusalem. As Zechariah said (8:3):

The Lord says: I will return to Zion and dwell in Jerusalem.

In order to retake the Golan Heights on Day 6 Israel needed to win against a heavily entrenched Syrian army of 75,000 troops. After 7 hours of heavy fighting Israel had miraculously gained control and the next morning instead of another day of fierce fighting, the Syrians fled frantically from the Golan leaving their weapons behind.

An Israeli platoon took heavy casualties and was left with only twenty-five men but they continued to charge Tel Fakhr in the Golan Heights, a heavily fortified Syrian position. The platoon did not stand a chance until a miracle occurred as a Syrian Captain ordered his men not to fire on the Israelis until they reached the wiring. The men told the captain it was too late; the Israelis were already inside with heavy

Syrian casualties. The miraculous victory of the Six Day War recaptured much of the land Israel has today.

During the Day of Atonement (Yom Kippur) in 1973 100,000 Egyptians invaded from the south and 1,400 Syrian tanks invaded from the north. Israel was caught completely off guard and outnumbered with most of its forces at home or in synagogues. Miraculously Israel won the Yom Kippur War and reached 20 kilometers into Syria.

During the Yom Kippur War, a small impossibly outnumbered Israeli force held back a large portion of the Syrian army, for four days in the Golan Heights. The Syrians had three infantry divisions and over 1,000 tanks. A Sergeant out of shells was ordered not to leave and miraculously the Syrians retreated just as the Israeli force was about to collapse. A Syrian soldier swears an army of Angels surrounded those few tanks Israel had and considering the rate of miracles surrounding the small country of Israel, that could truly be what happened in what is now known as, the Valley of Tears.

During the Gulf War in 1991, Iraq threatened to use chemical weapons on Israel which was not participating in the conflict. Iraq did bombard

Israel with rockets, but the chemical attack never happened. It is believed that because the usual wind patterns miraculously changed and blew east toward Iraq, the Iraqis did not want the chemical weapons to harm Iraqi citizens.

During summer 2015, it was discovered that Hamas had built tunnels in the Gaza Strip to invade Israel near the farming village of Sufa. The tunnel terrorists found only empty open land and a potential massacre was avoided as the terrorists were captured by the Israelis. The tunnellers did not know that the farmers harvested before a sabbatical year leaving the land to rest; ergo the tunnellers were not concealed by the high cover of wheat.[11]

Operation Entebbe or Operation Thunderbolt was a miraculous successful counter-terrorist hostage-rescue mission carried out by commandos of the Israel Defense Forces (IDF) at Entebbe Airport in Uganda on 7-4-1976. An Air France Airbus A300 jet airliner with 248 passengers had been hijacked by two members of the Popular Front for the Liberation of Palestine who wanted to exchange the hostages for 40 Palestinian and affiliated militants imprisoned in Israel and 13 prisoners in four other countries. The flight left Tel Aviv for Paris and landed in Entebbe, Uganda. Dictator Idi Amin welcomed the hijackers and moved the hostages to a disused airport building, the Jews were kept separately.

An Israeli transport plane carried 100 commandos over 4,000 kilometers (2,500 miles) to Uganda for the rescue operation. Some hostages had been released but the 106 remaining were under the threat of death; three were killed and 102 were rescued. Five Israeli commandos were wounded and one, unit commander Lt. Col. Yonatan Netanyahu, was killed (the older brother of Benjamin Netanyahu who became Prime Minister of Israel). All the hijackers and forty-five Ugandan soldiers were killed, and eleven Soviet-built MiG-17s and MiG-21s of Uganda›s air force were destroyed. Is the Israeli commando raid on Entebbe Airport a supernatural event or simply Jews risking their lives to save other Jews, or both?[12]

Jewish Achievements

With an estimated 7.4 billion people on earth, Jews comprise a mere .2 percent of that amount (about 14.2 million) and comprise large percentages in: Nobel Prize winners, Pulitzer Prize winners, Great Thinkers, Science and Medicine, Business and Finance, Entertainment Industry, Invention, Art and Literature, Chemistry, Economics, Literature, Peace, Physics, Physiology, and Medicine.

Between 1901 and 2015 CE, 201 Nobel prizes have been awarded to Jews, accounting for 23% of all Nobel prizes awarded (37% of American recipients) that is more than any other ethnicity.

Jews account for 53% of the recipients of the Pulitzer Prize for General Non-Fiction and 14% of the recipients for Fiction:

- Chemistry (36 prize winners, 20% of world total, 30% of U.S. total)

- Economics (31 prize winners, 39% of world total, 51% of U.S. total)
- Literature (15 prize winners, 13% of world total, 33% of U.S. total)
- Peace (9 prize winners, 9% of world total, 10% of US total)
- Physics (54 prize winners, 26% of world total, 38% of U.S. total)
- Physiology or Medicine (56 prize winners, 27% of world total, 39% of U.S. total)

Jewish Great Thinkers are known throughout the world:

- Albert Einstein established the foundation for much of modern physics and had a profound impact on everything from quantum theory to nuclear power and the atom bomb.
- Karl Marx the German philosopher, economist, and revolutionary, wrote *The Communist Manifesto* and *Das Kapital*, with the help of Friedrich Engels.
- Dr. Sigmund Freud was the founder of psychoanalysis and father of psychiatry.

Successful Jews in Business and Finance are also recognized very widely:

Haym Solomon and Isaac Moses created the first modern banking institutions, and the first department stores were started by Jews: B. Altman & Co. (1865-1990), Gimbels (1887-1987), Kaufmanns (1871-2006), Lazaruses (1851-2005), I. Magnin & Company (1876-1994), Mays (1877-2005), and Abraham & Straus, later A&S, (1865-1995).

Sears and Roebucks's mail order system was a merchandising revolution by Julius Rosenwald. Household names in men's clothing are Jews; Schaffner, Marx, Kuppenheimer, and Levi Strauss. Isadore & Nathan Straus (Abraham & Straus) became sole owners of Macy's in 1896.

Louis Santanel provided the funds for Columbus' voyage to America and English-Jewish financiers (Isaac Goldsmid, Nathan Rothschild, David Salomons, and Moses Montefiore) helped England become an empire while Armand Hammer (Arm & Hammer) originated the largest trade between the U.S. and Russia. Durable pants first used by 49ers during the American Gold Rush was invented by Levi Strauss.

Successful Jews in the Entertainment Industry are among the most famous names:

European Jews are the founding fathers of all the Hollywood Studios. Adolph Zukor built the first theater used solely to show motion pictures. Flo Zigfield of *Zigfield Follies* is the creator of American burlesque. Sherry Lansing of Paramount Pictures was the first woman president of a major Hollywood studio. Samuel L. Goldwyn & Louis B. Mayer (MGM) produced the first full-length sound picture, *The Jazz Singer.* Irving Berlin and George and Ira Gershwin are three of the most prolific composers of the 20th century. Harry Houdini (born Ehrich Weisz) is considered the father of magic and Steven Spielberg is arguably the most successful filmmaker since the advent of film. Many of the most famous actors, actresses, directors, producers, and musicians (Billy Joel, Neil Diamond, Paul Simon, Leonard Cohen) of the 20th and 21st century are Jewish.

Inventions by Jews are well known but rarely do people know who the inventors were:

The chief architect and engineer for the American Transcontinental railroad was Theodor Judah while the first gas station (1910) was opened by Louis Blaustein, the founder of Amoco Oil. In 1918 the first commercial parking lot in Detroit was opened by Max Goldberg. The creation of the NAACP had four Jews among the 60 multi-cultural signers in 1909. Emile Berliner developed the modern-day phonograph (gramophone) and his company became RCA while Louis B. Mayer (MGM) created the Oscar.

Some Jews are famous in Arts and Literature:

Marc Chagall (born Segal, Russia) is one of the greatest painters of the 20th century and the famous poem of Jewish Poet Emma Lazarus — *give me your tired ... your poor ... your huddled masses ...*appears as the inscription on the Statue of Liberty. Famed painter and muralist Diego Rivera played an important role in 20th-century art, especially as he was married to Frida Kahlo.

Famous Jews in the Medical and Life Sciences:

Dr. Jonas Salk created the first polio vaccine and Dr. Albert Sabin developed the first oral polio vaccine. In 1908 Dr. Paul *Magic Bullet* Ehrlich won the Nobel Prize for curing syphilis. The terms for antibiotics and vitamins were coined by Dr. Abraham Waksman and Casmir Funk respectively. Dr. Simon Baruch performed the first successful operation for appendicitis and Dr. Abraham Jacobi is considered America's father of pediatrics.

Some of the more notable Jewish contributions in the medical and biological sciences since the late 1800s (names of non-Jews are denoted with the superscript [+]):

The inventors of local anesthesia, Novocain, and penicillin usage were Carl Koller, Alfred Einhorn, and Dir Ernst Chain respectively. Sir Ernst Chain shared the 1945 Nobel Prize with Sir Alexander Fleming[+] and Sir Howard Florey[+]. Pancreatic dysfunction causes diabetes was discovered by Oskar Minkowski together with Joseph von Mering[+.]

Paul Ehrlich introduced the side-chain theory of antibody formation which evolved into clonal selection theory, the central paradigm of modern immunology. Ehrlich shared the 1908 Nobel Prize with Élie Metchnikoff*. Ehrlich is also considered to be the founder of modern chemotherapeutic medicine. Richard Lewisohn developed the sodium citrate blood storage technique (1913) and blood was able to be stored and banked for the first time. Lewisohn and Karl Landsteiner are two researchers most responsible for the invention of modern blood transfusions, estimated to have saved more than one billion lives since the 1950s alone, making it the single greatest lifesaving medical advance in history. Karl Landsteiner discovered the ABO and other blood groups and of the Rh factor receiving the 1930 Nobel Prize making blood transfusions safe for the first time. Landsteiner is also one of the giants of immunology for understanding the chemical basis of antigen-antibody interaction. Rosalyn Yalow and Solomon Berson invented radioimmunoassay and revolutionized clinical and research practice in such fields as endocrinology and blood banking. Yalow received the Nobel Prize in 1977.

Selman Waksman and Albert Schatz developed streptomycin receiving the 1952 Nobel Prize which created the first antibiotic effective against tuberculosis, a therapeutic mainstay. Herbert Fox and Harry Yale developed isoniazid the leading drug to treat tuberculosis.

Tadeus Reichstein isolated cortisone sharing the 1950 Nobel Prize with Edward Kendall[+] and Philip Hench[+]. The chemical synthesis of cortisone by Lewis Sarett[*], Max Tishler, and Carl Djerassi. The discovery of prostaglandins by M. W. Goldblatt also discovered by Ulf von Euler[+]. Arthur Eichengrun and Felix Hoffmann[+] developed aspirin.

Otto Loewi discovered neurotransmitters sharing the 1936 Nobel Prize with Sir Henry Dale[+]. The discovery led directly to the development of anti-depressants that includes Prozac, Zoloft, and Paxil and pain reliever acetaminophen (Tylenol).

Solomon Snyder and Hans Kosterlitz discovered endorphins and enkephalins. Louis Goodman,

Alfred Gilman, and Sidney Farber invented cancer chemotherapy in the 1940s. César Milstein was the co-inventor of monoclonal antibodies (anti-cancer drugs) and shared the 1984 Nobel Prize with Georges Köhler[+]. Gertrude Elion was the co-developer of 6-MP (6-mercaptopurine) combined with other drugs has provided cures for most forms of childhood leukemia (1988 Nobel Prize). Barnett Rosenberg discovered and developed cisplatin for a complete reversal in the prognosis for testicular cancer, now roughly 90% curable. Henry Kaplan revolutionized radiation oncology. Harold Varmus, Robert Weinberg, Michael Wigler, Bert Vogelstein, Arnold Levine, and others (1989 Nobel Prize) co-discovered and elucidated the role of oncogenes in human cancer. David Baltimore and Howard Temin discovered retroviruses and their associated reverse transcriptase enzyme (1975 Nobel Prize) implicated in AIDS and some cancers. The discovery disproved the central dogma of molecular biology. Jerome Horwitz, Samuel Broder, and Irving Sigal developed AZT, protease inhibitors, and other drugs used in the treatment of AIDS.

Rita Levi-Montalcini, Viktor Hamburger, and Stanley H. Cohen (1986 Nobel Prize) discovered the characterization of growth factors (nerve and epidermal) that play a large role in embryonic development and have potential in nerve regeneration, accelerated wound healing, and in the understanding and control of tumor cell proliferation. Alick Isaacs in collaboration with Jean Lindenmann[+] discovered interferon widely used in the treatment of multiple sclerosis, leukemias and lymphomas, melanomas, and hepatitis B and C. Shepard Shapiro developed Warfarin (Coumadin) for anticoagulant therapy.

Gregory Pincus, Carl Djerassi, and Frank Colton developed oral contraceptives. Otto Warburg*, Otto Meyerhof, Gustav Embden, Jacob Parnas, Sir Hans Krebs, Fritz Lipmann, Herman Kalckar, Carl Neuberg, Gerty Cori, Konrad Bloch elucidated the biochemistry of cellular metabolism, and all received Nobel Prizes. Baruch Blumberg and Irving Millman (1976 Nobel Prize) developed the hepatitis-B vaccine. George de Hevesy, Friedrich Paneth, Rudolf Schoenheimer, David Rittenberg, Martin Kamen, William Hassid, and Samuel Ruben invented radioisotopic tracer techniques used in radiocarbon dating. Hevesy and Paneth won the 1943 Nobel Prize in chemistry.

Phoebus Levene, Erwin Chargaff, and Rosalind Franklin provided the theoretical model and experimental data for Watson[+] and Crick[+] to determine the key components for the double helix model of DNA. Marshall Nirenberg and Har Gobind Khorana[+] broke the genetic code (1968 Nobel Prize). Stanley N. Cohen and Herbert Boyer's[+] invented gene splicing opening the new field of genetic engineering. Cohen and Boyer[+] were recipients of the US National Medal of Science and the US National Medal of Technology. Phoebus Levene, François Jacob, Sydney Brenner, Matthew Meselson, Sol Spiegelman, Sidney Altman, Sir Aaron Klug, Alexander Rich, Leslie Orgel, Andrew Fire, Gary Ruvkun, Roger Kornberg, Ada Yonath, and others discovered and elucidated the structure and function of RNA; all received Nobel Prizes. François Jacob, Walter Gilbert, Mark Ptashne, Andrew Fire, Gary Ruvkun, Howard Cedar, Aharon Razin, Michael Grunstein, and Michael Levine were co-discovers for the basic mechanisms of gene regulation. Jacob shared Nobel Prizes in 1965, 1980, and 2006.

I. I. Rabi (1944 Nobel Prize in physics) and Felix Bloch (1952 Nobel Prize in physics) discovered nuclear magnetic resonance (NMR) which led to MRI diagnostic imaging technique. Samuel Blum together with Rangaswamy Srinivasan[+] and James Wynne[+] invented LASIK eye surgery. Charles Kelman invented phacoemulsification cataract surgery, the most widely used worldwide. Basil Hirschowitz invented the flexible endoscope revolutionizing surgery by reducing the complexity and invasiveness of many surgical procedures. The invention led to the production of the first glass-clad optical fibers, revolutionizing modern telecommunications.

Paul Zoll and Wilson Greatbatch[+] invented the implantable and external cardiac pacemaker, the cardiac defibrillator, and the cardiac monitor. Michel Mirowski and Morton Mower were two of the four inventors of the automatic, implantable cardiac defibrillator. Henry Heimlich invented the Heimlich Maneuver.

Abel Wolman and Linn Enslow[+] invented the basic technique used worldwide for the controlled chlorination of drinking water resulting in a dramatic reduction in the incidence of such waterborne diseases as cholera, dysentery, and typhoid fever; arguably the single most important contribution to public health in the twentieth century.

In the 20th and 21st centuries Jews have played major roles in music as performers, conductors, and composers. Of the one hundred leading virtuoso performers of the twentieth century about 66% of the violinists, 50% of the cellists, and 40% of the pianists were, or are, Jews. Of the one hundred leading conductors of the twentieth century, about 25% were, or are, Jews. Among the leading classical composers, Jews are about ten percent, (most notable are Felix Mendelssohn, Jacques Offenbach, Gustav Mahler, Arnold Schoenberg, George Gershwin, and Aaron Copland). Jewish composers have also played predominant roles. Approximately 40% of the membership in the Songwriters Hall of Fame are Jewish.

The major Jewish figures in philosophy after Maimonides were Baruch de Spinoza, Karl Marx, Edmund Husserl, Henri Bergson, Ludwig Wittgenstein, and Sir Karl Popper (all of whom were estranged from Judaism). The Jewish representation of Great Philosophers is about 16% of the greatest figures in Western philosophical thought and in the twentieth century Jews are about 25% of the major figures.

Jews rank among the most well-known Psychologists and are 39% of the 100 Most Eminent Psychologists of the 20th Century: Sigmund Freud, Alfred Adler, Erik Erikson, Sandor Ferenczi, Anna Freud, Erich Fromm, Melanie Klein, Otto Rank, and Theodor Reik, Abraham Maslow, Ulric Neisser, Lev Vygotsky, Jerome Bruner, Herbert Simon, and Noam Chomsky.

The Founders of Modern Sociology also constitute some notable Jewish names: Emile Durkheim, Karl Marx, and George Simmel constitute three of the four individuals indisputably at the core of sociology's birth and growth. The fourth is Max Weber. Of the fifty preeminent sociologists discussed in Dirk Kaesler's *Klassiker der Soziologie* approximately 30% were or are Jewish.[13]

Summary and Conclusions

No people has ever insisted more firmly than the Jews that history has a purpose and humanity a destiny... The Jews, therefore, stand right at the center of the perennial attempt to give human life the dignity of a purpose.[14]

In the **Introduction** numerous notable gentiles wrote about the miracle of the Jews. For example: Blaise Pascal, the great French philosopher said the Jews are proof of the supernatural. Mark Twain called the Jews immortal. Leo Tolstoy called the Jews everlasting and an emblem of eternity.

In the **Abraham, Isaac, and Jacob** Chapter there were three famines sending the families of the Patriarchs and Matriarchs into exile from their homes. God promises the Land of Canaan to Abraham's descendants and a great nation from the descendants of Hagar and Ishmael. Abraham displays his deep loyalty to God by his willingness to sacrifice his son Isaac. After wrestling with an angel Jacob becomes Israel (*struggle with God*) and the Jacob's Ladder vision is seen as predicting the future exiles of his descendants from the empires of Assyria, Babylon, Greece, and Rome.

In the **Egyptian Bondage and Exodus** Chapter another Pharaoh enslaves the Hebrews and orders the killing of Hebrew first born sons. God speaks to Moses from a burning bush and tells him to return to Egypt and lead his people to freedom. After ten plagues ending with the death of firstborn Egyptian sons the Hebrew slaves are allowed to leave their Egyptian slavery.

In the Chapter **The Promised Land of Canaan** the *stiffed necked* Hebrews complained, built a golden calf, were involved in several rebellions and were punished accordingly. Joshua is chosen to succeed Moses and conquers the Canaanites. Joshua relates the story of Terah, the idolater and his son Abraham to the Canaanites establishing the Jewish tradition of never forgetting their heritage, history, Torah, God, and miracles. During the chaotic period of the Judges the Israelis became idolatrous and disobedient. In the period of the Kings the tribes split becoming the Southern Empire (Judah) and the northern Empire (Israel). The land was conquered by the Assyrians, the Babylonians, and the Persians before the Persians allowed the exiled Jews to return to Israel and rebuild Jerusalem's Second Temple. The Greeks conquered the Persians, and after a brief period of Hasmonean Hebrew control, the Romans took over killing and crucifying up to one million Hebrews before destroying the Temple in 70 CE which became the start of the longest and most brutal diaspora of 1,878 years.

The Chapter **Diaspora in the Common Era** documents the horrors, achievements, and miracles of the Jews from 70 CE through the founding of Israel in 1948 CE. From 70 to 1948 CE there were consecutive occupiers of the land who vilified, tortured, and killed many. Nevertheless, achievements were plentiful: completion of many sacred texts; the wisdom of the *Tannaim* and *Amoraim* rabbis; the creation of an eternal calendar. The horrors continued with near annihilation of the Samaritans, banning Jewish socialization, intermarriage, and conversions to Judaism. The highest Government and Church leaders were quoted vilifying the Jews and Judaism:

a perverse people; responsible for the death of Jesus; synagogues were (brothels, dens of vice, Devil's refuge, Satan's Fortress, abyss of disaster, places to deprave the soul).

Jews were massacred, could not hold public office, were not to have any authority over Christians, had to pay church taxes, and lacked civil rights. Nevertheless, they achieved success in maritime commerce, liturgical poetry, cloth dyeing, agriculture, silk weaving, assaying coins, banking, and service in government.

There were many forced conversions, exiles, many massacres during the Crusades, the Spanish Inquisition, and pogroms. Jews were expelled from the nations in Europe (some two or three times). Jews were forced to wear badges, hats, and special clothing. In Europe Jews comprised 50% of all medical doctors and the Church encouraged congregants to avoid them. Millions of Jews left Russia and Eastern Europe for the United States, Argentina, and Uruguay, the majority had prosperous successful careers. Jewish German citizenship was eliminated by the Nazi's Nuremburg Laws and the *Final Solution* slaughtered about 33% of all the Jews in the world.

During the numerous exiles and diasporas Jews were protected by other kings, princes, and bishops, because of the crucial services they provided in three areas: finance, administration, and medicine. Joseph Karo in Safed, Israel wrote the Code of Jewish Law - *Shulchan Aruch* in 1563 CE; the most widely accepted compilation of Jewish law ever written. There were some workers of miracles in the 17th and 18th centuries CE that culminated into Messianic movements.

The Chapter **The nation of Israel is born** begins with the Israeli declaration of independence in 1948 when seven Arab nations attacked to *push the Jews into the sea.* Greatly outnumbered 100 to 1, Israel's commander of operations Yigael Yadin described the victory: *It was a miracle*! Other miracles included: the 1967 Six-Day-War; the 1973 Yom Kippur War; Operation Entebbe or Operation Thunderbolt in 1976; the 1991 Gulf War. Noncombat miracles were also plentiful: Trees, fruits, and vegetables grow on sandy wastes and malaria swamps. New industries are everywhere. Many highways and pipelines have been built. Copper and iron mines along with agricultural settlements were established. The New York Stock Exchange lists more hi-tech companies from Israel than any other nation. When Israel airlifted thousands of

Ethiopian Falasha Jews in 1991 they became the only nation in recorded history not to enslave and export black Africans but to take them out for freedom and a better life in their Promised Land.

The Chapter **Jewish Achievements** defies reason due to the incredible volume of achievements in every area of human endeavor for a people that comprise only .2% of the world's population:

- Nobel prizes awarded;
- Jewish great thinkers - Einstein, Marx, and Freud;
- Well-known Psychologists and sociologists;
- Musical performers, conductors, and composers;
- First banking institutions, department stores, mail ordering, clothing, international trade, Hollywood studios, movies, burlesque;
- Inventions (transcontinental railroad, parking lots, gas stations, phonographs, Oscar Awards)

Medical and Life Sciences (polio vaccines; antibiotics; vitamins; appendicitis surgery; curing syphilis; pediatric medicine; local anesthesia and Novocain; safe blood transfusions; immunology; blood banks;

chemotherapeutic medicine; penicillin; streptomycin and isoniazid for tuberculosis; cortisone isolation and synthesis; aspirin; prostaglandins; neurotransmitters leading to anti-depressants and Tylenol; endorphins and enkephalins; nerve and epidermal embryonic growth factors; nerve regeneration; accelerated wound healing; control of tumor cell proliferation; Warfarin anticoagulant therapy; oral contraceptives; hepatitis-B vaccine; interferon for multiple sclerosis, leukemias and lymphomas, melanomas, and hepatitis B and C; anti-cancer drugs; cancer chemotherapy; most forms of childhood leukemia; cisplatin to cure testicular cancer; radiation oncology; role of oncogenes in human cancer; retroviruses and transcriptase enzyme to treat AIDS and some cancers; AZT protease inhibitors for treatment of AIDS; biochemistry of cellular metabolism; radiocarbon dating; radioimmunoassay in endocrinology and blood banking; experiments for double helix model of DNA; the genetic code; basic mechanisms of gene regulation; structure and function of RNA; gene splicing; nuclear magnetic resonance (NMR) leading to the MRI diagnostic imaging technique; surgical flexible endoscope that led to the production of the first glass-clad optical fibers; LASIK eye surgery; phacoemulsification for cataract surgery; cardiac pacemakers, defibrillator, and the cardiac monitor; Heimlich Maneuver; chlorination of drinking water and the dramatic reduction of cholera, dysentery, and typhoid fever.

Repair of the world (*tikkun olam*) is considered by many to be the mission of all Jews. With wars, hatreds, corruption, and worldwide criminal activity it may seem to many that the world is far from being repaired. However, people can and have repaired the world through their own spheres of influence, e.g., Harry Houdini (born Ehrich Weisz) entertained and inspired awe for thousands of people through his magic. Authors influence and inspire people through their writings. Religious leaders provide spiritual repair. The work of people in nonprofit organizations repair the world for all the children and adults receiving their services or by their advocacy for a better quality of life for everyone (global warming, free elections, democracy, education, equality, justice, etc.). Poets, artists, and actors repair the world for many people through their work. Businesspeople create jobs and employment so others can afford to live a productive life. Scientists and philosophers repair the world by always exploring better ways of doing and understanding things; they create, invent, and postulate theories for improved living. All people can be part of the world's repair through their personalities and interaction with others (kindness, caring, laughter, friendship, and helping). The Jewish achievements fulfill *Tikkun Olam* through entertainment, science, employment, and medicine where their achievements have saved billions of lives through blood transfusions and chlorinated water alone. Genetic research and therapy will eventually enable physicians to cure and heal people with individually prescribed remedies.

Books have been published regarding the miracles of the Jewish people mostly ascribed to practical historic considerations. Salo Wittmayer Baron credits Jewish survival to eight factors:

1. Messianic faith;
2. The doctrine of the World-to-Come increasingly elaborated;
3. Suffering was given meaning through hope-inducing interpretation of their history and their destiny;
4. The doctrine of martyrdom and inescapability of persecution;
5. Jewish daily life was very satisfying;
6. The corporate development and segregationist policies of the late Roman empire and Persian empire;
7. Talmud provided an extremely effective force;

8. Marriage was the foundation of ethnic, and ethical life.[11]

It is true that the belief in the coming of a Messiah is one of Rambam's Thirteen Principles of Jewish faith immortalized in his *Mishnah Torah*. The belief in a Messianic Age and a better world to come gave Jews and the entire world hope. The knowledge of long periods of Jewish suffering (famine, exile, enslavement, diasporas, and occupations by foreign powers) did require hope for survival especially considering historical redemption (survived three famines, over 200 years of Egyptian slavery, many exiles, and five foreign occupations over 1,000 years (Assyrian, Babylonian, Persian, Greek, and Roman). Martyrdom and persecution were continual and came to be expected. Tevye's family in *Fiddler on the Roof* beautifully exemplifies Jewish daily life during the third and longest diaspora; daily life was generally satisfying with periodic government persecution with pogroms and ghettoized living. Roman and Persian segregationist policies did allow Jews to pray, preach, and live with limited interference which was extended throughout the third diaspora. The Torah represents God speaking to the Jews and the world and the Talmud represents Jewish responses, interpretations, and commentaries; it was and is an effective force but studied and known to a minority of Jews. The commandment to be fruitful and multiply (Gen 1:28) could only be fulfilled through marriage and family. Judaism did transform from a centralized controlled religion in Jerusalem to a religion celebrated by small family units during the Babylonian Exile. It returned to a centralized religion when the Second Temple was completed, and the Jews returned from Babylonian exile; they had learned how to live and function without a central controlling authority in Jerusalem which they would utilize to survive in the Roman diaspora.

I think Baron's eight factors of Jewish survival are very compelling. If one does not believe in the supernatural, and/or Divine influence it is still difficult to reconcile Jewish survival. No other people or tribe has been vilified, persecuted, and slaughtered by the millions over thousands of years and survived. How could a tiny population of people be crushed by the most powerful empires in history (Assyrians, Babylonians, Persians, Greeks, and Romans) and not only survive as all the empires died but went on to incomprehensible successes. Does hope, the afterlife, family units, and the Talmud explain these miracles? It is possible although challenging to believe.

The challenge is as follows:

Jews returning by the millions from the four corners of the planet to the Promised Land after 1,878 years in exile and diaspora and activating conversational Hebrew as the national language; the return of swamps and deserts to fertile land for communities and their agriculture; the reforestation of the land by planting millions of trees based on ancient wisdom; the new mines dug for ores and metals based on ancient wisdom; how Israeli hi-tech companies on the New York Stock Exchange are more than any other nation in the world?

With the blood of Abraham, Sarah, Isaac, Rebecca, Jacob, Rachael, and Leah coursing through my veins how could I not be proud, honored, grateful, and awed knowing the history of my people...*Baruch Hashem!*

References

1. h t t p s : / / m f a . g o v . i l / M F A / M F A -
A r c h i v e / 1 9 9 6 / P a g e s / P r e s i d e n t
WeizmanSpeechBundestagJan2016-2019.aspx

2. https://www.jewsforjudaism.org/knowledge/articles/
quotes-about-the-jewish-people/

3. Terah's Family Tree https://en.wikipedia.org/wiki/
Terah

4. Rabbi Dr. Hillel ben David: *The Four Exiles*

5. Dunn, James G.; Rogerston, John William (2003).
*Eerdmans Commentary on the Bible. Wm. B. Eerdmans
Publishing* p. 545 ISBN 978-0-8028-3711-0

6. *Encyclopaedia Judaica.* 3 (2nd ed.). p. 27

7. **Jump up to:** *Second Temple Period (538 BCE. to 70 CE)
Persian Rule. Biu.ac.il. Retrieved 2014-03-15*

8. Naomi E. Pasachoff, Robert J. Littma. *A Concise History of the Jewish People.* **Rowman & Littlefield, 2005. p. 43**

9. h t t p s : / / w w w . j e w i s h v i r t u a l l i b r a r y . o r g / t h e - a n c i e n t - g r e e k s - and-the-jews-jewish-virtual-library

> **Jewish Encyclopedia:** *Rome: Early Settlement in Rome*

> **Smallwood Mary E. (2001).** *The Jews Under Roman Rule: From Pompey to Diocletian: a Study in Political Relations.* **BRILL. ISBN 0-391-04155-X**

10. www.jewishvirtuallibrary.org/byzantineempire

> **Eliyah's Forums** *A Brief History of 2000 years of Jewish Persecution* **7-25-1999.**

> **Birnbaum, David** *Jews, Church and Civilization* **New Paradigm Matrix: 6-10-2012**

11. **Benson Bobrick,** *Wide as the Waters: The Story of the English Bible and the Revolution it inspired.* **Simon & Schuster, NY, ©2001, p. 297**

> *Top 17 miraculous Israeli military victories.* **Israel Video Network, (5-20-2015)**

https://www.jewishvirtuallibrary.org/17-miraculous-israeli-military-victories

Baron, Salo Wittmayer: *A Social and Religious History of the Jews.* **Columbia University Press**

12. https://en.wikipedia.org/wiki/Operation_Entebbe

13. https://www.learnreligions.com/impressive-jewish-accomplishments-2076052

    www.bible411.com/bookletoffer/IsraelANationOfMiracles.pdf

    http://www.bibletoday.com/archive/israel_nation_of_miracles.htm#.Xs8M0zOSmUk

14. Guinness, Os: *Carpe Diem Redeemed: Seizing the Day, Discerning the Times.* **InterVarsity Press**, 2019 p. 18